JOHN X. JAMRICH:
THE MAN AND THE UNIVERSITY

Russell M. Magnaghi

 Northern Michigan University

Center for Upper Peninsula Studies
John X. Jamrich: The Man and the University
First Edition
ISBN 978-1-312-44521-5
Copyright 2014 By Center for Upper Peninsula Studies, Northern Michigan University, 1401 Presque Isle Ave., Marquette, Michigan.
Published in the United States of America by Center for Upper Peninsula Studies, Marquette, Michigan
Author: Russell M. Magnaghi
Editor: Ted Bays
Production editor: James Shefchik
The views expressed by the author are his personal views and not those of Northern Michigan University

Dedicated to
Northern Michigan University Administrators,
Staff, Faculty and Students during the Jamrich
Administration

Acknowledgments

This biography is the product of numerous people and departments. The Upper Peninsula and Northern Michigan University Archives is the best source of information on the history of the institution. The staff, especially Annika Peterson, reference assistant and archivist Marcus Robyns, have always been extremely helpful and knowledgeable of materials in their possession. Of special focus are the many oral interviews of the era: they provide insights on the Jamrich administration. More focused are the personal reminiscences of John X. Jamrich. Both he and his wife June have maintained an exemplary file of materials dealing with their lives and tenure at Northern Michigan University. I must not fail to note Mariam Hilton the author of *Northern Michigan University, The First 75 Years.* Her work is a wealth of information between two covers. I must also include my own reminiscences since I arrived on campus in September 1969 and have many memories of the Jamrich administration as a young faculty member. My work as University Historian has also produced, *A Sense of Time: The Encyclopedia of Northern Michigan University*.

Finally I have been greatly aided by Ted Bays, editor extraordinaire. He has provided valuable assistance and helped move the project along in a timely fashion. He deserves a great deal of credit for the final outcome. April A. Bertucci and Lara A. Clisch, the principal secretaries in the History Department, were extremely helpful preparing this manuscript for publication. The individual who facilitated the production of this biography is James Shefchik, a Northern alumnus who mastered the intricacies of publishing and brought the final version of the book to all of us.

Finally even with all of the documentation, interviews, reminiscences, etc., this is my work and there are bound to be human errors. Some readers may find that I am not critical enough on certain developments or that I left out material. These are my doing. All I can say is that this work is a base-line study and future researchers are encouraged to continue the study of the Jamrich administration and others. For now enjoy the story as it unfolds—the first biography of a Northern Michigan University president.

John X Jamrich. *All images courtesy of Northern Michigan Archives, Northern Michigan University.*

Table of Contents

Acknowledgments	v
Preface by President Fritz Erickson	ix
Introduction	1
Chapter 1: Childhood Experiences	5
Chapter 2: The War Years	11
Chapter 3: Marriage and Education	15
Chapter 4: Training for the Future, 1951-1958	17
Chapter 5: The Northern Challenge: Settling In	29
Chapter 6: Accreditation and Programs	35
Chapter 7: Faculty, Research & AAUP	55
Chapter 8: Sports and Athletics	63
Chapter 9: Bricks & Mortar	67
Chapter 10: Students & Alumni	73
Chapter 11: The Curtain Drops	79
Chapter 12: The Man and His Wife	85
Epilogue	93
Appendix I: Reports and Publications	101
Appendix II: Memberships	105
Appendix III: Other Activities	106
Appendix IV: Awards	109
Appendix V: Remembering the Man	110
Notes	114
Bibliography	118

Preface

I was honored to be chosen as president of Northern Michigan University in 2014. The position provides me with the opportunity to lead faculty, staff, retirees and alumni who really care about NMU students and their families, as well as to be engaged with Northern's dynamic and adventurous students themselves. NMU is known for its excellence in the classroom and throughout the overall student experience. It is also known for its can-do attitude and work ethic. So, when asked to become president of this fine institution, I felt and continue to feel privileged to fill this important role.

Dr. John X. Jamrich had the honor of being NMU's president for 18 years, which is the second-longest presidency in the university's history. During his nearly two dozen decades here, Northern experienced strong growth in enrollment, programs, research and community outreach. A lot of what is the foundation of today's Northern Michigan University was laid under the guidance of President Jamrich. In this book, Dr. Russ Magnaghi details the challenges and triumphs of the Jamrich tenure, of which there were many.

While I am new to Northern and have not had the opportunity yet to spend much time with June and John Jamrich, I am already incredibly impressed by what I've learned about the work they have done during Dr. Jamrich's presidency but even more so in the 30-plus years since his retirement. Both John and June, as well as their daughters, have remained engaged in the university, and we thank them all for their unwavering support. This book provides insight into the Jamrich family gifts given to NMU to assist various programs, such as those in the Music Department, and to the frequent interaction Dr. Jamrich continues to have regarding activities on campus.

Dr. Magnaghi provides a comprehensive overview of the lives of John and June Jamrich, which allows us to see how their own childhoods, family experiences professional endeavors would help shape the leaders they would become at Northern Michigan University and influence some of the decisions they made while at NMU.

The book is a great read about Northern's eighth president and his service to our institution as its leader from 1965-83 and as one of the school's biggest fans and strongest advocates ever since. It is a fitting tribute to Dr. John X. Jamrich.

Fritz J. Erickson, 15th President
Northern Michigan University

INTRODUCTION

Back in 2011 as the director of the Center for Upper Peninsula Studies, I discussed with then Professor David Haynes the idea of a series of base-line biographies of Northern Michigan University's president since Edgar L. Harden to the present. We decided not to go back beyond Dr. Harden because we did not have oral interviews of those earlier presidents nor did we have a body of personal documentation in the form of journals or correspondence. However a general study might be devoted to all of them.

So general criteria were developed for the creation of these biographies. We would look at the origins of and the influences on the lives of the presidents, the process they followed to become president of the institution, problems facing the university at their arrival, how their administrations developed given the outside forces at work, and finally what was their legacy and how have they been perceived given later developments.

However, before I go much farther I should inform the reader of my connection to the Jamriches. When I arrived on campus in September 1969 to teach in the History Department I was a new faculty member a few months out of graduate school in my late 20s. I had little interest in Northern's administration. President John X. Jamrich was a relatively remote figure whom I infrequently saw, but heard a great deal about through the faculty "grapevine." He was the president who chose to always wear a bow tie and was always seen formally dressed in a suit. There were apocryphal stories about him and the complaint by some faculty that most NMU publications carried his photo.

The years passed and soon it was the mid-1990s and I was now a senior faculty member. In this decade President William Vandament appointed me as University Historian. In this position as we moved toward the celebration of Northern's centennial in 1999 I was fortunate enough to have to delve into Dr. Jamrich's administration and life for centennial publications. I was there when much of what I write about took place, but I gave it little thought as I taught my students and conducted my research. As I learned more about Dr. Jamrich, I soon realized I was dealing with a highly savvy administrator, one who had worked his way up the ladder of success from humble origins, always assisted by his caring wife and family.

As I further developed this biography I was amazed to find how closely Dr. Jamrich worked with his staff, faculty, and students in the process of making Northern Michigan University the institution that it is today. As I ventured into reports, correspondence, oral histories, photographs, autobiographies, and newspaper accounts, I was nearly overwhelmed by Dr. Jamrich's deep concern and on-going love for the institution that was so much a part of his life for fifteen years and beyond.

Usually when a president leaves the university the door closes and that is the last that you see or hear of him. This certainly has not been the case with John and June Jamrich. For the last 31 years, they and their families have maintained a keen interest in and close ties with Northern and the Upper Peninsula. They have an abiding sense of time and place.

In retrospect one recalls "outrage" among many when the 1969 Instructional Facility was named Jamrich Hall in 1975, during Jamrich's tenure. At the time Dr. Fred Sabin, a member of the Board, said that he proposed and secured approval of that naming because it "reflected the Board's strong feeling for the superb job Dr. Jamrich has done for NMU." In retrospect the Board was not inaccurate in its analysis. John X. Jamrich's legacy outshines most presidents who have served Northern over the last 115 years.

It is hoped that these base-line biographies will provide current or future researchers with the initiative to pursue more detailed studies of the individuals or their administrations. One of the biggest problems in dealing with a president from the mid-twentieth century is the fact that individuals still alive who remember them, who ascribe and perpetuate myths and legends connected with them and thereby create a false perception of them. Many of the "legends" are widely perceived as reality despite the lack of footnotes or documentation. So this is a start to rectify that.

Before we go too far it is best to review the presidential history of Northern Michigan University going back to its founding on April 28, 1899 when Governor Hazen Pingree signed the bill that establish Northern State Normal School. Since that time there have been fifteen presidents of the institution holding office for a year or more and for eighteen years in the case of English-born James B. Kaye. Only one president, Judi Bailey was a female. Prior to 1963 the presidents were selected by the State Board of Education and were usually born and educated in the state of Michigan. This Michigan connection changed with the coming of James Appleberry and the succeeding presidents until the arrival of Fritz

Erickson in 2014. These presidents were directed by either the State Board of Education or the Board of Control, later called the Board of Trustees. They had to work within the parameters of these governing bodies while at the same time dealing with educational issues for the good of the students attending the institution. Furthermore, until the 1960s, Northern was focused on teacher education and had the John D. Pierce Laboratory School on campus where future teachers were trained in classroom settings. University presidents also have to deal with the state of Michigan appropriating the necessary funds to operate the school.

So these presidents are influenced by their backgrounds, personalities, education and earlier careers; external local, state, national and international events and forces; and finally the mandates set by the Board of Trustees. From this background, I will move forward into the life and times of John X. Jamrich, the eighth president of Northern Michigan University, who arrived in 1968 and retired in 1983 and thus is the second-longest president to serve after President Kaye, who administered the university for nineteen years.

Each president had a particular agenda given the times and circumstances. President Dwight Waldo (1899-1904), who got the institution started, hired faculty, sold the new institution to local students, and saw to the construction of the first buildings on campus. When he started his tenure he was called a principal. He and his family actually resided in the first dormitory. President James Kaye (1904-1923) saw the institution make some major developments with the construction of new facilities, the development of sports programs, and the introduction of the Bachelor of Arts and Sciences. It is interesting to note that retired president Kaye continued to teach at least one semester a year for the next decade. John Munson (1923-1933 was brought in to improve standards and saw the institution through the 1920s. Webster H. Pearce (1933-1940) saw the college through the hard times of the Depression and is the only president to die in office. Henry A. Tape (1940-1956) operated with a small staff and student body due to World War II but with the return of veterans saw an increased enrollment that swelled the student body. It was during his administration that Lee and Carey Halls were built, the first new buildings since 1915.

Edgar L. Harden (1956-1967) was told by the State Legislature to either close Northern or develop it as a first-rate institution! This he did on a grand scale and introduced the right-to-try policy that gave many students an opportunity to get a college education. In 1964 Northern

Michigan College became Northern Michigan University through the new state constitution. Unfortunately, many saw the institution as a university on paper but not a university in fact. Before much could be accomplished to change that, a number of issues developed that brought turmoil to the campus. President Harden resigned and Ogden E. Johnson was interim president from September 1967 to June 1968. John X. Jamrich (1968-1983) then implemented many of the ideas introduced by Harden and made NMU a "university in fact" during his fifteen year tenure. John X. Jamrich, then, is the subject of this biography, the first in an on-going series.

CHAPTER 1: CHILDHOOD EXPERIENCES

Complex individuals must be understood to better appreciate them and their achievements. So it is with John X. Jamrich, an individual who played such an important role in the educational history of the state of Michigan. As we course through his life we will see many influences that made him what he was and thus shape his impact on subsequent history. The first three ingredients in a recipe for success as President of Northern Michigan University are his upbringing, education, and early career.

John Jamrich's childhood itself had three distinct phases: Birth and two years in tiny Fruitport, Michigan; the next eight years in his mother's birthplace, little Drietoma, Slovakia; then public school and church school in the large and vigorous ethnic enclaves in the Milwaukee, Wisconsin suburb of Cudahy.

<u>Slovakia and Immigration</u>

In order to better understand the Jamrich story it is important to introduce Slovakia to the reader. The Slovaks are a Slavic people who became attached to the Kingdom of Hungary by the Middle Ages and thus were ruled by a Magyar people. There were cultural tensions between these two nationalities. Modern Slovakia was known as Upper Hungary and had no precise geographical definition nor a distinct legal, constitutional or political status within Hungary. In the late nineteenth century the Hungarians tried to "Hungarianize" Slovakia by forcing Slovaks to learn Hungarian in school and naturally there was little opportunity for Slovaks within the kingdom. In the 1870s the first Slovaks began to immigrate to the United States. Between 1880 and the mid-1920s, approximately 500,000 Slovaks immigrated to the United States from the Austro-Hungarian Empire. The high illiteracy rate of the immigrants reflected their rural background and farming heritage and the fact that the Hungarians discouraged the development of literacy among the Slovaks. As a result it was common for Slovak-Americans to settle in areas of steel manufacturing and coal mining, where unskilled labor was in demand. The younger generation was encouraged to secure jobs rather than advance in society. Few Slovak-Americans entered the professions.

But the Jamrich story—especially the John X. chapter—contradicted the usual story of Slovak-Americans. It goes back to European origins and immigration to the United States in the first decade of the twentieth century.

John Jamrich's father Jan left Kálnica in Slovakia and came to the United States in about 1910. Like many immigrants to the United States, he came to avoid conscription into an imperial army to which he owed no particular allegiance. Until 1918 the Slovaks and the Czechs or Bohemians were part of the Austro-Hungarian Empire and then were united as Czechoslovakia. How Jan secured the means to leave his homeland remains a mystery. First he settled in Bridgeport, Connecticut, which had neither steel mills nor coal mines. Within the first week of his stay in Bridgeport, he was walking the streets trying his luck at running into a job opportunity. He told the story that one day he happened to stop in front of a bakery to "get the aroma of fresh-baked bread and cakes" and admire them in the window. The owner of the bakery came out and asked him if he "knew how to bake bread." Jan did not speak any English at the time, but nodded in the affirmative. The owner took him right into the bakery, put an apron on him and set him to work on the bread-baking shift. Fortunately, Jan had paid very close attention to and participated in the bread baking back home in Kálnica. In her reminiscences, John X. and June's daughter Marna recalls watching her grandfather Jamrich baking bread at their home in East Lansing during their Michigan State University tenure.[1]

Next, Jan moved west to Watervliet-Troy, New York, north of Albany, where many Eastern Europeans had settled. John's mother, Maria Mudry-Sebik, had emigrated unaccompanied at age 15 from the Slovakian village of Drietoma and settled in Troy as well. She had to fulfill her binding arrangement as a maid with a Jewish family; they had provided the dollars for the trip. Jan and Maria met at one of the Slovak gatherings at Troy and they were married in 1913.

The newly married couple, Jan and Maria, now Americanized to John and Mary, decided to move farther west to the Milwaukee suburb of Cudahy, Wisconsin, a meat-packing town populated by Slovaks. Soon after Ann, was born. Then, apparently because they knew Slovaks in the Muskegon, Michigan area directly east across Lake Michigan from Milwaukee, they purchased a 40-acre farm in Fruitport, Michigan, southeast of Muskegon.

John Jamrich was born in Fruitport on June 12, 1920. During the Fruitport years, John's father worked in a Muskegon Heights foundry, riding a bicycle several miles to and from work. His mother took care of the family and, like many immigrants, developed a small farming business. Mary churned butter by hand and delivered butter, eggs and vegetables with a horse and wagon and sold these items to a group of steady customers in town.

In 1922, after two years in Muskegon Heights, the second phase of John Jamrich's childhood began when his parents returned to Slovakia. Mary wanted to live close to her family—mother, father and several brothers—in Drietoma and they bought a house and adjoining 80-acre farm on the outskirts of town. The basic amenities were unlike life in America: outhouse, well, no electricity, big woodstove for cooking and heat, and space in the stove's surrounding structure for two people to sleep. John's father spent most of his time back in the U.S. earning a better living. He was not happy in Slovakia as life even with American-earned money was not as easy as he had imagined. Finally, after his last trip to the United States in 1926, he wrote to tell the family to return to America. Now John X.'s father had to become a citizen so his wife and children could return.[2]

The seven years spent in Slovakia had a profound effect on young John and contributed to his education, in literally a "school of hard knocks":

> We owned a cow for our milk; chickens for eggs, couple of hogs for the usual November kill to have meat and bacon, and sausage for the winter. We owned a flock of geese; special occasions we would have roasted goose or duck. The cow and the geese were taken (during the summer) out to pasture some distance away. I would join several other youngsters with their cows and we would go to the pasture area every day. One such "out to pasture with the geese" experience is still clear in my memory. The geese were doing well, swimming down the stream toward our home. Unfortunately, one of the geese decided to exit the group and waddle well off to the side of the creek. I took a stone, with the idea that a casual throw would scare the goose back [to] the others. To my consternation, the stone hit the goose right on the head and killed it. Naturally, I brought the dead goose home; it would be dinner in a day or so. But my dad, who happened to be visiting us from America for a few weeks, really got very angry that I killed the goose. Eating geese was strictly for holidays and special

occasions. That's when I received a strapping that I still remember.³

John's youthful years in Slovakia had a number of positive impacts on him. Young John's schooling in Slovakia took place in a one-room school house. The teacher had no formal training but was simply the oldest lucid resident of the village. One dividend of living in Slovakia was that a few relatives who were musicians got John interested in music, which would blossom when he returned to the United States. Also the Slovak experience made him multi-lingual. Slovak was the basic language spoken, but there was opportunity for contact with Czechs, Polish, and German folk.

When the Jamrich family returned to the U.S. in June 1929 - briefly to Michigan, then to Cudahy— nine-year-old John's unfamiliarity with the English language and his rudimentary schooling landed him in the first grade. Bigger than his classmates, he had to sit side-saddle at his desk. Fortunately, patient teachers and his own aptitude for language and learning lifted him quickly to the grade level of his age cohort and into a desk that fit. Later he worked part-time in the neighborhood meat market where Slovak was more frequently spoken than English. The lasting impact of this "there-and-back" experience provided him with an appreciation of interpersonal relationships and friendships; and his personal work ethic was influenced by those early days in Slovakia and then reinforced by living through the Depression. Finally the importance of and respect for family, two of his lasting "life patterns," were instilled by that experience as well.⁴

The Jamrich family fit well into the Slovak-Czech-Polish neighborhoods of greater Milwaukee. The foundries, factories and meat-packing plants provided jobs, although during the Depression John remembers his father often working in a foundry in South Milwaukee only one day a week, with a paycheck of $5 to $10 for two weeks. He also found a job in a Cudahy Brothers meat-packing plant, "a most interesting facility." As John has written:

> It was certainly true that the plant processed everything but the squeal from the hogs. . . . my dad was employed, because of his mechanical ability, in the fertilizer department. That department processed all of the "throw-away" insides of hogs and cattle that were slaughtered at

the plant. The drying kiln was a cylindrical, cast-iron container about 30 feet long. At times, when it became inoperable and needed interior repairs, my dad had to climb in there for the repair, a task usually requiring several hours in the over 100 degree heat.... For my dad and uncles [two of Mary's brothers from Slovakia roomed with the Jamriches], the treat at the end of a hot working day in the summer was to come home and send me for a couple of lard pails of beer.... It was a good trick on the part of my dad and uncles to smear a bit of lard on the inside of each pail so that the saloon keeper could not foam up the beer; the lard assured a full pail of beer.[5]

Survival during these years was a community affair. The Jamriches borrowed the newspapers—"especially the comics"—from their neighbors, the Witkowskis, who also gave them use of their phone. A neighborhood wine-press processed grapes into wine; the grapes and other fruit came across Lake Michigan on the "fruit boat." Home-made beer, hidden under the cellar steps, emitted the occasional muffled "pop" when an over-pressurized bottle cap or cork exploded from fermentation. Also fermenting in a large crock in the cellar was cabbage for sauerkraut, sliced by a manual slicer operated by young John. Backyard gardens produced vegetables, berries, and potatoes and carrots, stored under the porch in piles of sand. When the carrots attracted rabbits, father John snared them for the stew pot.[6]

Young Jamrich's association with poultry continued in Cudahy: One of my regular chores practically every Saturday was mother sending me to the Cudahy Flour and Feed Store, located about four blocks away on Munkwitz Ave., near Packard Ave. Mother would give me specific instructions for buying the chicken for the Sunday soup and meat. At the store I had the pick of 40 or 50 chickens. Having chosen one, I took it home and it was my additional responsibility to kill the chicken and to dip it into scalding hot water. Then I would pluck all the feathers out. All of this work was done in our basement. The next step was to gut the chicken and prepare it for mother's inspection. If I did not pluck it clean, I had to go back downstairs and work on it some more. . . . During the Depression years, even the chicken legs were included in the food dish in the center of the table.[7]

Religion played an important part in the lives of the Jamrich family. The Slovak Lutheran churches—services, scripture, confirmation classes and song books in Slovakian—were named St. John's, in both Cudahy and Kenosha. Socialization by grade school youths involved ethnic solidarity imparted by religious training. After the English-speaking public school day, John and his Slovak classmates attended an hour of church school, conducted in the Slovak language. He recalls Sunday services conducted in Slovak for two of the three services; a few years later, one service was in Slovakian, two in English; and eventually all in English.

Schooling

One public school duty led to Jamrich's life-long avocation of music:

> I had the privilege, when I reached the 7th and 8th grades, to play a classical record for the entire school every morning—through a system that Mr. Hogue, the principal, had constructed—and to give a brief description of the music. I started piano lessons even though we did not have a piano at home. I would come early to school and practice on the old piano in the school auditorium. That I was able to do as long as I cleaned all the blackboards in our homeroom. The cost of the piano lessons was 25 cents.[8]

He also found time to take clarinet, flute and violin lessons.

Jamrich graduated from Cudahy High School in 1939 with the highest grade point average in his class of 200 and was designated valedictorian. He won a full tuition scholarship of $37.50 to Milwaukee State Teachers College [now University of Wisconsin at Milwaukee] to pursue his goal of teaching mathematics and music at the high school level. He augmented that munificence by working summers at the Cudahy meat-packing plant for 25 cents an hour. After a year at Milwaukee State, Jamrich shifted to Ripon College for two years; he finished his undergrad degree in Physical Sciences at the University of Chicago in 1943.

CHAPTER 2: THE WAR YEARS

From the chastening effects of a foreign childhood, emigration, a Depression upbringing in a working class neighborhood, and hardscrabble college financing, John Jamrich then found himself in a world war. He also found a middle name. And all along he had been finding a life partner.

As the John Jamrich story unfolds he notes that he was a college drop-out:

> I remained at MSTC [Milwaukee State Teachers College] for the summer of 1939, and the 1939-40 academic year. In the meantime, my good friend Don Barrer had gone to Ripon College on a private scholarship. He continued to nag me about transferring to Ripon because he thought that it had such an excellent mathematics and physics program. It also had a minor program in music. . . . It was during the fall quarter of my junior year (1941) and the beginning of the second quarter (January 1942) Don Barrer and I, watching all of the other fellows leaving [to join the military], decided to make application for the meteorology program of the Air Corps. We mailed our applications to the University of Chicago, MIT, and New York University. We were getting rather anxious about being accepted, as the weeks rolled by. In a daring move, even though we had not heard anything from any of the three universities, Barrer and I simply quit school.[9]

However they were both accepted. Jamrich went to Chicago and Barrer to New York University.

Jamrich and his classmates jammed a 3-year program into nine intensive months of study and training. Of the 85 cadets in the program, Jamrich was one of three without a B.S. degree; the rest had at least a Masters, and ten had a Ph.D. Academic rigor was not the only challenge. As cadets, he and his classmates wore the Air Corps uniform—wool. Fine in the fall, winter and spring, but extremely uncomfortable in the summer. Nonetheless, "elegant" living quarters, good food, and a world-class cadre of teachers left an overall positive impression on John, as did a classroom move: The cadets vacated Ryerson Hall to make room for a team of top-notch scientists, whose work culminated under Chicago's abandoned Stagg Field on December 2, 1942 with the world's first man-made nuclear chain reaction, later deployed, of course, as the bombs that ended the war in the Pacific.

As a graduate of the University of Chicago Meteorology program, Jamrich was commissioned as a Second Lieutenant in the U.S. Army Air Corps, as the Air Force was called then. That, and his facility with an Eastern European language, made him an ideal candidate for a most unusual assignment.

The Gilded Age phrase-maker Charles Dudley Warner, cribbing from *The Tempest*, tossed off an enduring witticism when he observed in 1850 that politics makes strange bedfellows. So does war. In World War II, the United States found itself allied with the Soviet Union in opposition to Nazi Germany. As part of the Lend Lease program, the U.S. gave airplanes to the Russians. American fliers ferried the planes westward across North America, north to Alaska; from there, Russian pilots took over and flew the planes across the Bering Strait and the vast expanse of Siberia, to the German front even farther west. That icy region required accurate weather forecasts to navigate safely, and thus John Jamrich found himself bunking with some odd comrades.

As he later recounted, "I felt that this was a bi-national honeymoon, but I never had the feeling that the wedding had taken place." International affection (or lack of it) aside, Jamrich developed a satisfactory working relationship with the Russian pilots, mechanics, and commanders: "But the pilots, for whom this temporary flight duty of ferrying planes was their rest and recreation from the battles of the Russian front, and I became very good friends as they developed an almost complete dependence and confidence in my forecasts. . . . The pilots were much like ours—carefree, but loyal." Paid in U.S. currency, the Soviet fliers bought personal items at the PX and sent the rest of their money back home to support the war effort. "They were generally heavy drinkers. Often, they brought over their own supply of vodka. But, they clearly had an eye out for the welfare of their country and the people back home."[10]

Sometimes Jamrich flew with the Soviet planes in an accompanying B-25, from Fairbanks to Nome, Alaska and across the Bering Sea as far as their first stop at Welkal in Siberia. The legendary bomber led the other planes up over the cloud deck when it obscured navigation over the Bering Sea. The eight or nine thousand American planes ferried to Russia included P-39 and P-63 fighters, the A-20 low level attack bombers and the bigger high altitude B-25, "their favorite action aircraft, although they always went back to the DC-3 as the most dependable for transport."[11]

To complete at least two flights, in the long summer days at that latitude, and perhaps three, meant that the pilots would have to be awakened very early, about 2 a.m. to get to the flight line. However that meant that John was required to be awake even earlier to prepare the forecast so they were not being wakened only to face a "no flight" day. If there was an early flight, John would then be able to get back for some shuteye and be available for the forecast for the second and/or third flight. This made for a long but rewarding workday, but as John recounted, "summer was not for hibernation!"

We have more details from Jamrich, the weatherman in war-time Alaska:

> But there was a hidden problem in the spring and fall (and sometimes in the summer) weather situation at the Ladd Field [Fairbanks] location. Given a damp day, followed by a cool night, there would develop a morning fog along the river and over the field. The trick was to figure out some scheme to be able to forecast when that fog would break up so that flights could take off. After some careful data gathering during the first spring, I was able to design a nomogram that enabled us to predict with some accuracy when the morning fog would break up in the sunlight.[12]

Jamrich undoubtedly gained the appreciation of the hard-pressed Soviet pilots for giving them a few extra hours of sleep. For his accurate weather forecasts, he was presented with an official Soviet Air Force citation in 1945. In 1977, Jamrich was given a Commemorative Medal by the Soviets.

During his military service Jamrich acquired his middle name. U.S. Air Corps paperwork required a middle initial. Jamrich had no middle name so he just made an X. When further pressed for a complete name, he randomly selected "Xavier."

CHAPTER 3: MARRIAGE AND EDUCATION

Another name change bloomed during the World War II years. John X. Jamrich married June Ann Hrupka, and June Ann Hrupka Jamrich has been his steadfast helpmate and life partner ever since.

They knew each other from the Slovak neighborhoods in Wisconsin. In fact, June Ann's family came from John X.'s father's home town of Kálnica in Slovakia. June Ann's mother Anna Kukucka Hrupka had come to the U.S. in 1912, stayed with an older sister in the Troy, New York area, went on to the Slovak enclave in Chicago, and there married John Hrupka in 1919. They moved to Kenosha in 1921; John worked in the Nash automobile factory. In her reminiscences in the *Our Family Circle* manuscript, June Ann Hrupka Jamrich relates vivid memories of her parents' business ventures, especially the Soft Drinks Parlor, so named during Prohibition. It was, in fact, a tavern, and when raided by the constabulary it was locked up, one of many "Padlock Cases" in that and other ethnic neighborhoods during Prohibition.

After high school, June Ann went on to Russell Sage College in Troy. Home in Kenosha to work in the summer of 1943, she spent time with John X., home on leave from Alaska to attend the funeral of his mother. Then John X. went back north, June Ann went back east, and the letters between them began to fly back and forth. They were married in June of the following year. After a brief honeymoon at a Kenosha hotel, they again went back north and east to the military and to college, respectively. In August of 1945, they managed a true honeymoon getaway to the historic King Edward Hotel in Edmonton, Alberta, Canada.

John X. Jamrich received his military discharge in 1946, the same year June Ann graduated from Russell Sage College. They then settled in Cudahy with John X.'s father. June employed her college marketing degree at the Gimbels department store, and later Schuster's, in Milwaukee; John, after a brief stint as a Northwest Airlines weather forecaster back in Alaska, reunited with his wife in Cudahy and started classes at Marquette University in Milwaukee—essentially the true beginning of his career in higher education and administration.

Higher Education at Last

John X. Jamrich had hitchhiked back and forth from Ripon to his father's Cudahy home. Now the commute to Marquette University, straight west on Wisconsin Avenue in Milwaukee, was accomplished by bus. But Jamrich's next stop in his preparation for a career in higher education required a car—always a memorable step for a young married couple. John X. and June Ann bought a Nash coupe in 1948.

After passing the exams for his Master of Science degree at Marquette University, Jamrich wound up in Chicago again, or at least the Chicago area. He had decided to pursue the doctorate degree, and started at the University of Wisconsin at Madison, renting a room there and commuting back to Cudahy—and June Ann—on the weekends. Then his old pal Don Barrer again urged Jamrich to transfer, this time to the Ph. D. program in Math at Northwestern University in Evanston, Illinois. By happenstance, Jamrich acquired an appointment as Assistant Dean of Men, a position that came with free room and board. To better acquit himself in this role, Jamrich took a class in Counseling and Student Personnel work. "That step, in fact, proved to be a turning point in my academic and professional career in the years to come. What eventually happened was that I became enamored, as I always had been, with the teaching profession. Over the ensuing year or two, I added to my academic program more from the College of Education than from the math department."[13]

In the course of his years at Northwestern, Jamrich scored the highest in history (up to 1950) on the all-day Miller Analogies Test, and secured a graduate student assistantship that included the supervision of all of the student teachers in the Evanston public schools. He typed his Ph.D. dissertation on an old manual clunker in an older wooden building on campus, and, fearing fire might reduce his efforts to ash, made carbons of every page and kept them in the trunk of his car.

CHAPTER 4: TRAINING FOR THE FUTURE, 1951-1968

Jamrich passed his exams, scored one of the highest, up to 1950 on the Miller Analogies Test, and received his Ph.D. in Education in June of 1951. After exploring a few job opportunities, he and June chose a position at Coe College in Cedar Rapids, Iowa. With the $5,000 annual salary, Mr. and Mrs. Jamrich bought furniture and moved into their first real home—a spacious rent-free perquisite for the Dean of Students—near the campus. The home was also near the hospital. When the Jamrichs' first child June Ann, was born Sept. 30 that year, mother June A. grabbed her suitcase and walked to the hospital. Among the important purchases to furnish the Cedar Rapids home, none ranked higher than a grand piano and a high-fidelity record player, reflecting John X.'s esteem for music as a good influence in a child's upbringing.

At Coe College, Jamrich encountered the first episode of a recurring theme: declining enrollments. The dormitories were half empty. To supplement the college president's vigorous recruiting efforts, Jamrich added on-campus attractions, for both students and parents: Freshman Orientation, with parental attendance encouraged; Parents Day weekends; personal involvement in student activities, with John X. and June Ann both taking part. May Fete, an enduring Coe tradition, saw the Dean, his wife, and four-year-old daughter June Ann participating their last year there.

A brief note on names: The names John Jamrich and June Ann Jamrich do double duty until altered. John X.'s father, Jan, became John Jamrich after a few months in the U.S. Rather than use "John Sr." and "John Jr." it seems handy and readily comprehensible to have used "Father Jamrich" and "Young Jamrich", and mostly, "John X." Likewise, John X.'s wife has been June Ann until the birth of their first daughter, also named June Ann. In "Our Family Circle" the historical/biographical monograph, John X. employs "June" or "June A." for his wife, after the birth of June Ann.

The Jamrich' second child, Marna Mary, was also born in Cedar Rapids, on January 29, 1954.

Coe College Dean of Students John X. Jamrich attracted the attention of other small colleges, and one in particular came calling, with an offer that steered John X. toward his successful career in the Faculty,

Curriculum and Development aspects of university administration.

Doane Years

In 1955, Jamrich received a visitor from Nebraska. The president of little Doane College in Crete, Nebraska, 20 miles from Lincoln, interviewed John X. and offered him the position of Dean of Faculty, "to provide academic and administrative leadership." Jamrich later wrote:

> In retrospect, it seems that my intuition was prompting me to recognize that, perhaps, university and college administration would be my professional career. I took on a leadership role in the Nebraska Association of College Presidents. Even before my in-depth involvement with the Michigan Survey of Higher Education, my mathematical background provided a basis for analyzing certain quantitative aspect of the college operations.[14]

The Doane College President Don Typer, heavily pre-occupied with fund raising to supplement tuition income and maintain accreditation, delegated responsibility across many administrative fronts to his new Faculty Dean: curriculum, faculty, admissions, student recruitment, even athletics. Having been a state quarter-mile champion in high school, John X. served as tennis coach at Doane.

President Typer stocked his Board of Trustees with people of financial wherewithal to match their education background and church affiliation. The Board members were most generous with their support as the college had been operating with some decreases in enrollments for a few years. The result was a short fall in the annual budget for the preceding year. The meetings were an interesting experience for the young new administrator. At the annual meeting when the deficit came to the surface, several of the Board members simply took out their checkbooks and each one wrote out a check so that the total of the checks would balance the budget.[15]

Doane's affiliation with the Congregational Church carried some force in the Jamrich family's daily life. When beset by diaper duty, June A. hung the cloth diapers out on the clothesline one Sunday and promptly received a visit from the wife of the Vice President for Finance, who informed the newcomer that Doane mothers did not hang laundry on a Sunday.

One elliptical connection at Doane led to the next big step in John X. Jamrich's steady march toward a university presidency.

Michigan Legislature

In 1954 Jamrich attended a 5-week workshop on higher education at the University of Michigan. There he met James Doi, Assistant to the Executive Director of the Board of Higher Education in New Mexico, Dr. John Dale Russell. A year later, Dr. Russell called John X., and Michigan beckoned. Russell was by then working a few days each month as a consultant to the Michigan Legislature. His task: A massive Study of Higher Education throughout the state. His immediate need: A fulltime Assistant Director.

The Jamrich family "...huddled for a careful consideration of the options." Dean Jamrich was also a tenured faculty member at Doane. But the Michigan Study was just entering a data gathering and analysis phase, a perfect fit with Jamrich's skills. With a leave of absence from Doane, the Jamriches moved to Michigan.

John X.'s travels did not end when they got to Lansing. He visited every one of the ten state supported colleges and universities, the 50-plus private colleges and the twelve junior/community colleges in Michigan.

A small residence on Sparrow Street near the State Capitol building, gave Jamrich a short commute to work and his daughters' handy access to schools, the Barnes Avenue Park, and a nearby grocery store. Eventually June A. got a teaching job in the Lansing Public Schools after earning her teacher's certificate at Michigan State University. Here again, family life benefited from the "team approach" emphasized by John X. in his recounting of each stop on his progress to the Presidency of NMU. With John X. often on the road and working weekends and holidays to gather and organize data for the Legislature, parenting often fell to June A.

> Jamrich recalls his first unofficial encounter with his new boss: We were to meet, at the small office area occupied by the Study staff in the capitol building, on the first Monday in July of 1957. June and I decided to attend church on the Sunday, just before I was to meet with Dr. Russell. At church, we were ushered to a pew near the front of the church. Sitting next to me was a gentleman who took quite an interest in the church bulletin, just before the church

service began. I noticed that he was actually "editing" the bulletin, correcting some of the typographical and spelling errors in it. What a surprise it was to meet the real Dr. Russell for the first time on Monday and realize that he was the gentleman sitting next to me in church that Sunday.[16]

In two years John X. Jamrich produced a 14-volume study of Higher Education in Michigan that other states used as a model for their own assessments, and that put Jamrich in a perfect position to move on to jobs at nearby Michigan State University that in turn served as the final springboard to his university presidency.

But first he had to get the lead out. From a small office in the Capitol building, Jamrich and Dr. Russell's team moved up to the fifth floor, which housed tons of old hot-lead printing plates used to produce decades of legislative reports. The floor sagged from the weight, which, removed, gave the Study team ample work space. Here Jamrich's skills in data collection and collation came to the fore. Because Dr. Russell came to Lansing only two or three days each month, Jamrich had several weeks to assemble material for his Director to review and edit. Then Jamrich wrote the final reports. He also made personal contact with most of the higher education community of the government and the entire state:

> This experience provided in-depth acquaintance with the members of the Legislature, the Office of the Governor, and the administrative officials at the ten state-supported institutions, the fifty or so private colleges and more than a dozen community colleges. . . . Most importantly, it was an in-depth acquaintance with the substance of college and university operations, curriculum, finances, student affairs, etc. Not until my subsequent positions as Professor of Higher Education at Michigan State, Associate Dean at Michigan State, and finally President of Northern Michigan University, did I fully realize the significant role of the Study experience.[17]

The concept itself anticipated a trend at top-notch universities. Undergraduate and graduate programs in Institutional Research met the growing demand for skills in this aspect of university administration. Among the many applications of Jamrich's Study, the Michigan

Constitutional Convention of 1961-62 adopted its recommendation that state colleges and universities be "imbedded"—that is, mandated,—in the new state Constitution.

    The Study's substance addressed every aspect of higher education: An overview of all the public, private and community colleges; general population distribution; population projections and student enrollment projections; curriculum; student services; research; adult education; physical plant and facilities; projected need for more classrooms and other facilities; faculty—age, salaries, years of service, projected need for more faculty; institutional finances—debt, endowment, scholarships; control and coordination among institutions; analysis of possible need for more institutions; and a need for a third medical college.

    Jamrich's work on the Study brought him to the attention of Michigan State University President John Hannah, a vigorous and foresightful leader. Mindful of the self-scrutiny trend in high education, he offered Jamrich the directorship of MSU's Center for the Study of Higher Education. Jamrich also held a professorship in the same field. He later (1961) became Assistant Dean of the College of Education, and then (1963-68) Associate Dean.

    Along the way, Jamrich declined other job offers: director of the Illinois Board of Higher Education; another to direct the establishment of Southern Illinois University at Carbondale; President of the University of South Dakota. President Hannah coached Jamrich in a strategic job offer rejection: Vice President of NMU. "Dr. Hannah speculated that something better might turn up." It did: the NMU presidency.

Grand Valley

    But before that final step in Jamrich's career, he notched several noteworthy accomplishments downstate. First came the Grand Valley report. Essentially, Grand Rapids businessman and civic leader William Seidman[18] founded Grand Valley State College. However he had lots of help, especially from the Survey and Report conducted, written and presented by John X. Jamrich in 1959.

    It was hard to resist the momentum of, first, a growing community with visionary leaders, and, second, a man with data. Although apprised in 1956 of demographics that virtually demanded another four-year college in the area, the Grand Rapids Board of Education and the Michigan Legislature only took action on that need when nudged by Seidman and his committee of local and Lansing leaders, armed with the

Russell Report and further bedrock data presented by John Dale Russell's full-time Michigan Study Director, John X. Jamrich. His work on the Higher Education Study for the Michigan Legislature had noted a need for another four-year institution in Michigan. As the second-most populous urban area in the state, Grand Rapids seemed a logical location.

But how to proceed? Grand Rapids Community College could be expanded; both the University of Michigan and Michigan State University bid to expand their powerful fiefdoms; or a new college could arise. The Final Report for the Michigan legislature (assembled and written by Jamrich, then edited and approved by Russell) bristled with the customary Jamrich array of compelling data:

> The forecast predicted that "enrollments would move from the 134,604 actually attending in the fall of 1956 to 164,770 in 1960, to 217,057 in 1965, to 289,979 in 1970, and to an estimated 340,000 in 1975." (p. 11-12 of the Final Report) . . . We agreed to include the following statement: "A superficial review of the Michigan situation leads to the conclusion that the most likely location for another State-controlled college is Grand Rapids."[19]

John X. Jamrich never settled for "superficial" so he sent out 12,000 questionnaires in an eight-county area around Grand Rapids and got 10,000 back. Parents and students from the 2nd, 10th, and 12th grades expressed their likelihood of college attendance and their career preferences. This critical survey in 1959, enabled by the state legislature's Seidman Resolution and manned by MSU's loan of Jamrich to conduct the work, substantiated the Grand Valley team's claim of need and gave specific direction to academic programs.

> Throughout my work on the survey information, I adhered to the basic notion that the new college, if one were warranted, should reflect in its curriculum/academic programs content that will meet the expressed needs of the student and parents in their responses to the questionnaires.[20]

Not everyone joined the team right away, one influential area citizen ", . . . chastised me for proposing and supporting this entire concept. . . and furthermore, providing the facilities of a new college right there in the Grand Rapids area 'would enable any and all types of students, regardless of ability, to pursue a higher education.'" No doubt the specter of such benighted social elitism spurred Jamrich to continue NMU President Edgar L. Harden's egalitarian "right to try" approach 10 years later.

With Jamrich's data as a foundation, the Michigan Legislature passed House Bill 477 in 1960 and Grand Valley College was born. Site selection followed in 1961, earth broken near Allendale, west of Grand Rapids in 1962, a Board of Control appointed and a President selected. Then in 1968, new college President Dr. Arend D. Lubbers ushered in the full flourishing of Grand Valley State University. Today's modern campus hosts 24,000 students. In 1985, on the twenty-fifth anniversary of its charter, Grand Valley presented John X. Jamrich with an Honorary Doctor of Laws Degree, President Lubbers doing the honors personally. Dr. Jamrich was extremely proud of this award, making him an honorary alumnus of the institution he helped create.

Michigan State University

While working on the Grand Valley project, Jamrich continued to work for Michigan State and continued there for another nine years, rising steadily in the College of Education—as at NMU, the dominant area of undergrad instruction and enrollment.

Their East Lansing years also kept all the Jamriches busy in school. June Ann, Marna Mary and Barbara Sue kept Mrs. J busy ferrying children to school and related activities, while she pursued and earned a teacher certificate and then substituted as a teacher in Lansing Public Schools. The family also spent time each summer by Lake Missaukee near Lake City, where other MSU staff had built summer cottages. Then John X. and June A. found a beautiful 40-acre farm in Vermontville, complete with its own little lake and a Ford tractor.

With three daughters in the area public schools, Mrs. Jamrich found herself quite active in school matters. She served as the president of the Whitehills P.T.A. And she was a girl-scout leader for the Central School Girl Scout group. June also was a member of the Lansing Women's Club and the Michigan State University Faculty Folk. She also served as the president of the 9-hole Faculty Golf Group. The golf was played on the MSU courses, always kept in A-1 condition. And she was active in the Figure Skating Association.[21]

Dean/Professor Jamrich employed his growing battery of skills in higher education assessment by consulting for institutions from Lansing to Virginia to Nigeria as seen in Table 1:

1967-1968	Member, Association for Higher Education Program Planning Committee
1967	All-University Committee on Undergraduate Education, Michigan State University
1966	Consultant, Michigan Department of Education
1966	Consultant and Director of Facilities Study for South Carolina Commission on Higher Education
1966	Director of Facilities Study in Michigan's State Institutions
1965	Staff Consultant and Director of the Study of Capital Outlay Needs for the Virginia Commission on Higher Education (Dr. Russell)
1965	Consultant to the State Board of Regents of Ohio (Dr. Millett)
1964	Consultant to the Ford Foundation on the University of Nigeria
1962-1963	Director, Study of Capital Outlay Needs for Ohio's State Institutions of Higher Education
1962	Accreditation Examiner and Consultant to the North Central Association of Colleges and Secondary School
1962	Consultant to Educational Facilities Laboratories, Inc.
1962	Director, Survey of Higher Education in the Saginaw Valley
1962	All-University Committee to Study Economics of College Students and the Out-of-State Students (MSU)
1961	Study of Physical Plant Needs for Council of State College Presidents in Michigan
1960-1961	Studies of Higher Education in New York (Heald Committee)
1958-1961	Director, Committee on Liberal Arts Education (North Central Association)
1958-1961	Professor of Higher Education; Director, Center for the Study of Higher Education (MSU)

In between these projects and administrative responsibilities, Jamrich and his family found time to plant trees on their Vermontville property.

World of Music

Music, next only to his family and career, has run through John X. Jamrich's life as a sustaining and expressive force. In Cudahy, young Jamrich's elementary teacher Miss Avis Roth encouraged him in piano at Washington School. The Jamriches did not have a piano at home so young Jamrich came to school early to clean the blackboards and smack the chalk dust out of the erasers, to earn time at the old auditorium upright.

He began piano study with Steve Jursik, the organist at Cudahy St. John's Lutheran Church. He also studied with Charles Burgess. In high school solo and ensemble competitions, Jamrich won a first place rating on piano with a Chopin scherzo. He also won a first on clarinet. His senior year at Cudahy, he entered a national composition competition sponsored by *National Scholastic* magazine. His string quartet for two violins, viola and cello took second place nation-wide. At the Cudahy High School graduation ceremony in 1939, he played in the orchestra and also played a clarinet-flute duet with Kathryn Petri.

Jamrich also studied with Norbert Schneider at the Wisconsin Conservatory of Music. Schneider was a pupil of Josef Lhevinne, the great Russian pianist and teacher who escaped Europe after World War I and came to the U. S., eventually teaching at The Juilliard School. Lhevinne was once a guest at Schneider's house; he talked with and played for eight of Schneider's students, including Jamrich. Lhevinne favored Chopin and played the Waltz in C# minor. "Also he made the point that 'music' should be uppermost in the mind of the performer. He pointed out that 'I can play the Chopin Minute Waltz in 59 seconds, but where is the MUSIC?'"[22]

Jamrich attended Chicago Symphony performances at the Pabst Theater in Milwaukee. He especially remembers an encore by Poldi Mildner of Chopin's Octave Etude to make up for imprecise execution of octaves in a Brahms Sonata earlier in her concert. (An on-line video of Mildner, the blond Viennese phenomenon, shows an energetic performance of this Chopin piece.)

Jamrich continued his piano studies at the Milwaukee State Teachers College under the tutelage of Howard Stein. He chanced into a generous benefaction when he answered a newspaper advertisement for landscape maintenance at the home of a Mrs. Gysin. This kind lady encouraged Jamrich to practice on the Gysin's Steinway grand, paid for lessons from John Carre in Racine, and accompanied Jamrich to those lessons in the Gysin convertible.

Jamrich also benefitted from other teachers at MTSC: Hugo Anhalt, orchestra director; and Milton Rush, a musical genius who taught composition and harmony and directed the Milwaukee Symphony.

Home to work for the summer from Ripon College in 1941, Jamrich appeared as the guest conductor of the Cudahy Municipal Concert Band for the Fourth of July festivities. Jamrich had been studying orchestra conducting with Ed Zielinski, a flautist with the Milwaukee Symphony who had taken master classes in conducting from Frederick Stock of the Chicago Symphony. Jamrich also directed the church chorus at the German Lutheran church in Ripon. Many of the anthems there were sung in the German language, which Jamrich understood and spoke.

While at the University of Chicago learning weather forecasting in the Army Air Corps program, Jamrich maintained a practice routine on piano. At the graduation ceremony at International House, a young pianist performed Tchaikovsky's B-flat Concerto; Jamrich played the orchestral accompaniment, transcribed for piano.

While at NMU, Jamrich had occasion to visit the Kaufmans at Granot Loma Farms, northwest of Marquette toward Big Bay. "Mrs. Kaufman was seriously into music; she genuinely appreciated my coming over to the Lodge and playing on the grand piano." Eventually, the Kaufmans sold the Jamrich's 300 feet of lake-frontage on Saux Head Lake, "where we built a cottage and spent many, many enjoyable days during our 15 year tenure at Northern."[23]

During retirement, Jamrich has continued his musical avocation in Jacksonville, Florida. As with his education and career, he followed up on a chance encounter to open a new avenue of opportunity.

During the first week of February 2003, John X. experienced another interesting and attractive opportunity, quite by accident, so to speak:

> During the preceding year, we had been utilizing, of course, the medical facilities of the Mayo Clinic . . . . In our walk through the Cannaday Building, we noted the addition of a new grand piano. In fact, a slight detour into the Kinne Auditorium revealed the fact that there was also a new piano, a Steinway grand. One of the desk volunteers

indicated that both pianos had been donated by a Dr. Kinne rather recently. I inquired whether anyone was playing these instruments. The reply was that they had just stood there for some months as elegant pieces of furniture. But, I was told that if I were interested in volunteering, perhaps to play the lounge piano, I should proceed to the Volunteer Office in the Davis Building. In that office I happened to meet Dixie Thalmueller, one of the volunteers. She had the responsibility of coordinating the music volunteers for the Humanities in Medicine Program recently initiated by Mayo Clinic. Her response to my question whether anyone played those two new pianos was: "You're just the person we're looking for." She went on to explain that Mayo Clinic had just recently initiated a program entitled: Humanities in Medicine, designed to provide works of art, sculpture, and hopefully music. Would I be interested in playing appropriate music in the Cannaday Lounge? I gave an affirmative answer. That led to setting in motion my formal induction into the Mayo Volunteer Organization. A day or so later, I began regular performances in that lounge, playing four times each week for about an hour. In 2006, I was designated as Pianist in Residence at the Mayo Clinic.[24]

CHAPTER 5: THE NORTHERN CHALLENGE: SETTLING IN

A change of era took place in June 1967 when President Edgar L. Harden, the force behind the development of Northern Michigan College to university status, resigned. There were some major problems facing Northern Michigan University. Harden had resigned due to a personal difference between President Harden and one or more Board of Trustee members. Furthermore, President Harden had terminated Dr. Robert McClellan, professor of History under questionable circumstances and the result was turmoil on campus between faculty and students versus the President and the Board of Trustees. A law suit was brought against the administration on May 22, 1968 and the Board decided to reach an out-of-court settlement before the upcoming new academic year.

On June 1, Jamrich concluded his service to Michigan State University and planned to spend several weeks vacationing with his family before the move to Marquette. The Board's request to solve the legal problem became his main concern during the month of June. In the past Northern had few legal problems and relied on a local attorney for advice, which was all that was required. However the McClellan situation was serious and complex. To cope with it properly Jamrich decided that the University should engage a prestigious law firm on a continuing, consulting basis. The Board of Trustees agreed and approved the firm of Miller, Canfield, Paddock & Stone of Detroit. Richard Jones of that firm became the first and "almost full time" legal counsel. Then Jones and Jamrich started to work on the problem in late May and by June 26 they finalized a settlement that was agreed to by Professor McClellan and the Board of Trustees. The first problem was rather quickly solved.[25] It is interesting to note that despite Dr. Jamrich's successful solution to the McClellan controversy, his efforts were generally downplayed or ignored and, in some quarters, he was even blamed for the controversy.

In the late 1960s throughout the United States former state teacher's colleges were being upgraded to multi-disciplined universities with growing enrollments and related problems. At Northern similar problems would have to be dealt with. On campus, dormitories had been constructed for incoming students, the Learning Resources Center was under construction and ground had been broken for a new classroom building—all good. However a number of problems dealing with faculty and programming faced the institution. Between 1965 and 1967, eighty-three faculty had left Northern, a major concern. The Climate of Learning Committee of the Faculty Senate appointed a sub-committee to discover the reasons. They discovered a national concern by faculty to "seek direct participation in the formulation of policies and rules that govern their performance." Further, through questionnaires, the Committee found that 50 percent of the former faculty had left "Northern because of the administration, academic freedom, salary, their department chairman exercising little influence over the dean, and their dislike for the Common Learning Curriculum."[26]

The years of turmoil that ended in June 1968 now allowed the re-design of University programs, facilities and faculty, which progressed from its College and Teacher's College image into the actual University status prescribed in the new state Constitution. The Board of Trustees had been seeking a new president and in May 1968 announced the selection of John X. Jamrich. Although there is documentation as to the thinking of the Board at that time, it is obvious by their choice of Dr. Jamrich that they wanted to address the problems facing the institution. In many respects he was the obvious choice for a new president. He came to the position with a strong background. From his years of past experience he had very strong ideas of where higher education in America should be going in general and the role Northern, now a middle-sized, multipurpose institution, should be playing. In this regard, he had a national and international reputation as a much-sought-after consultant on higher education. He arrived at Northern having most recently served as Associate Dean of the College of Education at Michigan State University. His experience at MSU included directorship of the Center for the Study of Higher Education. Finally his landmark achievement, in the eyes of many educators and legislators, was study of the educational needs of the Grand Rapids area, Michigan's second-largest city, and the creation of Grand Valley State University. He was thoroughly prepared for his new assignment. Dr. Jamrich realized that Northern would have to go from the university on paper to a university in fact. This would be his next concern as he entered the presidency, having been appointed in March 1968.

We have seen that he had the experience, skill and expertise to enter the fray and bring about a change. As he later noted, "One of the major factors considered by the Board of Control [name since changed to Board of Trustees] in appointing me as president of the University was my extensive set of experiences related to higher education in general and institutional operations and administration in particular."

Now his task was to implement these ideas for change. He quickly "prepared a careful analysis of the status of Northern and set forth a realistic plan for the coming decade, a plan that would contribute significantly to the university status." In his inaugural address he stressed the point that the successes of his administration would occur only if every member of the faculty and staff "worked together toward appropriate goals designed to meet the needs of our students." He and the Board agreed that Northern must become THE institution of higher education in the Upper Peninsula, providing for the needs of all students, of all ages, to meet their individual needs and aspirations in the broadest sense of the word. His mantra, "Working to Put Tomorrow in Good Hands" became the University's guiding theme.

President Jamrich's changes for Northern were foretold by a glimpse of his philosophy of management as presented to the faculty convocation in September 1968. There would be transparency in the general conduct of university and academic affairs. He would introduce a cabinet-style of governance rather than the traditional presidential system of executive leadership. Finally, new and more rational decision-making would be introduced.

President Jamrich was a man with deep insights into higher education and understood that he would have to work closely with faculty and staff. As Miriam Hilton noted, "One of his first actions as president was to appoint faculty, administrative and student members to serve on three task forces. These groups were charged with studying and evaluating concerns in the areas of academic governance, student rights and responsibilities, and the overall future of the University." It all rested on Jamrich's first endeavor: establishing a cabinet style of governing and guidance that featured transparency of decision-making within orderly, codified procedures.

To make all of this work, administrative changes were undertaken and two new vice presidents were added. Dr. Jack R. Rombouts became Vice President for Administration and Secretary to the Board of Trustees. An affable individual from Iron River, Michigan, Dr. Rombouts brought to this position a broad background in education, having at one time been Deputy Superintendent of Public Education for Michigan. Instead of reporting to the president, the directors of Admissions, Institutional Research, Security, Alumni Relations, Athletics, Communications, Campus Planning and Development, and Research and Development would report to Dr. Rombouts. There was a new Vice President for Students Affairs, highlighting Dr. Jamrich's concern for students. Dr. Allen Niemi was promoted from Dean of Students to Vice President for Student Affairs. Reporting to him were Career Planning and Placement, the Health Center, the Counseling Center, and the Dean of Students. Dr. Jacob Vinocur, who came from Michigan State University, was promoted to the new position of Vice President for Academic Affairs. Now he oversaw the Registrar's Office and other academic matters including the Library and the Learning Resources Division. President Jamrich found Leo Van Tassel, who had been with Northern since 1946, thoroughly acquainted with the University's budgetary, business and finance picture and persuaded this capable man to remain as Vice President for Business and Finance. Claude Bosworth remained as Vice President for Continuing Education and Extension, former known as Public Services Division. An alumnus, Dr. Roland Strolle, was named Dean of Graduate Studies and, with Dr. Bosworth's sudden death in 1970 suddenly became Vice President for Continuing Education and Extension. Dr. Lowell Kafer was promoted to Dean of Students and in 1971 Dr. Robert Glenn became Dean of the College of Arts and Sciences and later would become provost.

In two new areas of expansion, Nursing and Business, there were changes. Mrs. Margaret Rettig, who had activated the Nursing program, went from Director to Dean of the new School of Nursing; and Dr. Donald H. Hangen came from California to become Northern's Dean of Business and Management. Personnel were set for the new administration to work towards a successful future.[27]

The next important move taken by President Jamrich was to give faculty, staff, and students opportunities for input into the decision-making process, in keeping with recommendations of the Task Force on Academic Governance. The University Advisory Council with representatives from the Academic Senate; the Administrative/Professional Staff Association, which had been given Board recognition in 1970; Associated Students of NMU; the Clerical/Technical Staff Association, recognized in 1972; and the Service Staff—all met regularly with the President. There was also a Task Force on Student Rights and Responsibilities and a third Task Force on the Future of the University among other things dealt with life on campus.

In that vein, the two other task forces—the Task Force on Student Rights and Responsibilities, and the Task Force on the Future of the University—indicate President Jamrich's scope of planning. The turbulent

1960's made student participation advisable; long-term success made future planning mandatory.

In typical Jamrich fashion, the University developed "The Development Plan 1968-1980" which created a set of goals for the future of the University: 1. instruction of knowledge and skills; 2. providing a liberal education with training for specific careers; 3. supporting research and scholarship; 4. public service, especially to the Upper Peninsula; and 5. providing a cultural center for the Upper Peninsula. With special consideration for U.P. high school students, President Jamrich, also aware of state-wide trends in other universities, wrote:

> ...The University has attempted to evaluate the potential of applicants in such a manner as not to exclude from the opportunity those high school graduates who may not have performed well in their high school years, but who evidence emerging potential and motivation to profit by a college education. This is particularly important in view of the changing picture of enrollments and admissions at the several large universities in Michigan which, by virtue of their missions, provide broader opportunities for graduate work in research, thus limiting their ability to take undergraduates in response to the needs of the state.[28]

CHAPTER 6: ACCREDIATION AND PROGRAMS

<u>Nursing and Allied Health</u>

After Northern gained university status in 1963 and more students were attracted to the institution, there was a demand for new courses that would lead to the world of work. During the Jamrich administration there were a number initiatives that brought to campus a variety of new programs and courses.

According to Dr. Jamrich, his first order of business was academic programs – the curricula. The formal accreditation of Northern's major program areas was the central consideration as the University sought to improve existing programs and initiate numerous new academic majors and degree programs. Northern's accreditation efforts were successful in each program for which there was a requirement.[29] The University received full accreditation by the North Central Association of Colleges and Secondary Schools.

First there was the health care arena to deal with. Since the late 1960s, Marquette General Hospital had grown from the consolidation of several local medical care facilities into a highly regarded regional medical center. At the same time a growing nationwide shortage of nurses that threatened the very survival of many health facilities.

Having been made aware of this growing crisis, Dr. Jamrich directed a major expansion in NMU's nursing programs. Until 1968, the university did not have a four-year nursing curriculum. Changes began to take shape in the general field of health care on campus. First at a basic level, student health care. On July 1, 1969, Barbara Lyons, M.N. became director of an on-campus medical staff that included three physicians, ten nurses, eight clerks, and a pharmacist. An expanded clinic was housed on two floors of Gries Hall and included 18 infirmary beds, 12 examination rooms, office and pharmacy. By 1973, when the campus health center began charging minimal fee-for-service rates to those it served, an average of 120 students per day were receiving treatment for problems ranging from the flu to minor recreational injuries. A student Health Insurance Program was instituted to cover all treatment fees for a small annual premium.

This development was part of a large health care development taking place on campus and ultimately affecting the actual structure of the university's academic program. In 1968, the newly established School of

Nursing and Allied Health Sciences enrolled 35 students in a four-year training course for the first time, and this number grew over the years to 800 students, of whom 80 percent were in the nursing program. A true professional with an agreeable personality, Margaret Rettig served as the school's first director. By 1972 the Jamrich administration recognized the need to restructure its health care curriculum. The School of Nursing was expanded to include the Department of Speech Pathology and Audiology and several Associate Degree programs in the allied health field. To ensure high-caliber students, new admission standards were established and a 2.5 minimum grade-point average was set as a requirement for upper-level enrollees. Such improvements led to a coveted accreditation by the National League for Nursing. As a result of these advances, Rettig was promoted from Director to Dean of the School of Nursing, a position she ably exercised until her retirement on June 30, 1983.

Growth in NMU's medical offerings under Jamrich were not indiscriminate. "We established the Bachelor's Degree in Nursing, while still retaining the Licensed Practical Nursing Program." Jamrich recalled that Northern had "an opportunity to absorb a two-year nursing program when St. Luke's Hospital closed its school, but we decided, after reviewing the national scene, not to do so and to retain the Licensed Practical Nursing Program and undertake what has turned out to be a very successful effort in the area of baccalaureate (four-year) Program in Nursing." As a result, this program expanded very rapidly and quickly served the needs of the Upper Peninsula. The plan was for Northern's nursing courses to qualify graduates to become licensed as practical or registered nurses through State Board Examination and to earn the Bachelor of Science in Nursing. Speech Department courses led toward a Master of Arts degree in Speech Pathology. Associate degree programs prepared graduates to become Medical Laboratory Technicians or Radiology Technicians. In regard to the nursing core of the program, Jamrich noted that it was "very successful; the demand is very high. In fact, we can't produce enough nurses to meet the demand at the present time."

The Medical Technology Program was added, which provided both the Associate Degree and the Bachelor's Degree in this field. As the emerging health care needs of the Upper Peninsula were recognized, Northern established the Community Health Program. Through this program, senior student nurses were located in "health care stations" in Marquette County where they provided primary care screening clinics for blood pressure and diabetes screening, as well as for related health problems.

In 1975, recognizing the increasing complexity of the nursing profession, Northern took steps to provide course work beyond the baccalaureate degree level. The University began its approach to establishing a Master's program by joining with Wayne State University in a cooperative Master's Degree offering. Eventually, Northern offered that degree on its own.

During the Jamrich presidency Marquette General Hospital and Northern developed a close working relationship that benefited both parties. NMU students gained valuable clinical experience and MGH employed trained professionals from their ranks. NMU students in the health and business fields participating in internships at MGH have found them a good learning experience. Foremost among the training programs was the Baccalaureate Nursing program, "the largest and fastest growing in the university," as noted by Betty Hill, Dean of the School of Nursing and Allied Health Sciences in 1983. Hill continued, "Students from all four branches of our department have had clinical experience at MGH. Clinical experience is not only helpful, it's absolutely essential to the program."

Thus health education grew steadily at NMU since it began with a Practical Nursing Program and a graduating class of six in 1948. By 1983 the program consisted of four departments—the Baccalaureate Nursing, Practical Nursing, Communication Disorders, and Medical Technology departments—which offered a wide range of programs, including a special program for registered nurses (R.N.) who wish to obtain a bachelor's degree.

Hill stated, "President Jamrich has been a very active supporter of our nursing program. The highlight was his support of our national accreditation efforts. It took much central support." The program received national accreditation in April of 1981. "I think he considers the Baccalaureate Nursing program one of his major accomplishments," recounted Hill.

Another area of cooperation between MGH and NMU was the Emergency Medical Technician (EMT) classes offered through Northern's Department of Allied Health. Paramedics from MGH had taught EMT classes since 1978. In addition to textbook instruction, students gained exposure to clinical settings in the MGH Emergency Department and other areas of the hospital. Students also rode with the crews and gained invaluable experience in the field. It is required by law to have clinical experience, but these internships taught more than the law requires.

Other fields of study at Northern benefitted from the MGH-NMU connection. Students in the business field had opportunities for practical experience at MGH. The Office Administration program at NMU placed interns at MGH at the rate of two per semester. They could work in Human Resources, Accounting, Purchasing, and other business offices throughout MGH. As a result a number of interns were subsequently hired by the hospital. The general MGH employee can further their education by taking courses at Northern and a passing grade allowed a tuition reimbursement.

Summing up the MGH-NMU relationship, MGH Executive Director Robert C. Neldberg said, "Over the years, both Marquette General Hospital and Northern Michigan University have undergone great changes in growth and development. The continuing close relationship brings us together as partners in education and health care training." This relationship also provided health care workers to serve facilities through the Upper Peninsula—President Jamrich's ultimate goal.

In the beginning the Communications Disorder program was small and little known. Because Professor Lon Emerick had achieved a national reputation in this area the University decided to expand the program. His expertise and insights provided the impetus for strengthening the program. The audiology testing program and the clinical speech therapy services were developed on a regular outpatient basis. By 1975, Northern was recognized as a major diagnostic center for communication disorders. The following year, the graduate-level curriculum in Speech Pathology and Audiology was added. The Cleft Palate Clinic had been established in 1974. The staff developed internships at several Upper Peninsula hospitals.

An important program established in the Jamrich administration in 1973 was the Premedical Program and Premedical Advisory Committee. As a result of the high standards of this program, Northern students have earned one of the finest reputations in the Midwest. Against odds of acceptance that ranged from one in 20 to one in 56 applicants, ten of Northern's pre-medical students in a class of 13 were accepted for medical school. Between 1973 and 1980 over 50 students were accepted into medical schools. As of the date of publication, this program continues to produce these very positive results.

School of Business and Management

The management consulting firm of Cresap, McCormick and Paget developed a study in 1967 and using the results of this study, the School of Business and Management undertook the expansion and strengthening of both curriculum and faculty. The school made a triple thrust into the business world with departments in Accounting and Finance, Management and Marketing, and Office Administration and Business Education. All three departments rapidly added new programs and developed thorough curriculum changes. Two programs led to a master's degree.

Two special developments took place around the school. Upper Peninsula banker and philanthropist Sam M. Cohodas donated a gift of $250,000 to create a chair for a professorship in banking. And the Business Executive-in-Residence Program brought nationally recognized executives to Northern's campus.

The Business School was built on a changing curriculum encircling a solid core with flexibility to meet the changing needs of the students and the business community. The faculty increased from 22 to 32 within the decade and many had doctoral degrees and were publishing books and articles.

The School of Business not only trained students to enter the world of work, it also reached out to serve community needs. The School accelerated this outreach program with the establishment of a Business Development Center in 1979. The programs coordinated by the Center included: 1. Conferences and seminars co-sponsored by the Small Business Administration and the Marquette Area Chamber of Commerce; 2. Executive development program; 3. Faculty consultant referrals; 4. Special education programs and services of community interest.

Computers

During the Jamrich administration and partly because of his background in mathematics and with a personal and professional interest, Northern entered the computer age. Despite financial constraints NMU developed outstanding programs in computer science, robotics, and high technologies. What was brought to campus at that time seems primitive by today's standards, but the foundation was set. Fifty computer terminals were available to students in computer classes with plans to double in the next five years. Industry and Technology got into manufacturing engineering technology using robots. New and improved equipment was ordered and put into place on campus. English, Sociology and other departments were using computers. The Writing Workshop used computers to help students with their basic grammar, usage, and punctuation. Apple computers first appeared on campus at this time. This introduction and use of computers was later expanded into a cutting-edge program that, still today, makes Northern one of the few campuses in the country where all students and faculty have access to a lap-top computer.

Criminal Justice

Northern's location includes community resources comparable to a metropolitan area, with industrial firms that require security guards, a state prison, state police crime lab, and a rural crime scene. The only thing lacking is the high city crime rate. This, too, is an asset. It offers an opportunity for the study of criminal psychology. As a result the University was in an ideal location for a Criminal Justice program.

The Criminal Justice program was divided into three parts: Private Security, Corrections, and Law Enforcement. The department also established a Criminal Justice Training Center to better serve the law enforcement community. The program was built around a small, cohesive staff and adjunct instructors. The latter include attorneys who instructed classes in both criminal prosecution and defense. In 1980, Northern was still the only institution in the state of Michigan to offer two- and four-year courses in Criminal Justice. At that time, plans were made to request funding for a master's program in this field. As a result of this program some 550 students were majoring in Criminal Justice.

Fine Arts: Music, Drama, Art

As the University developed, President Jamrich was concerned that a central core of the program become a quality liberal arts curricular offering. As a result he designated a faculty committee to undertake a careful assessment of this aspect of the program and to seek appropriate revisions where indicated. The areas of Fine Arts—music, drama, and art—were the early focus of his attention.

Faculty with appropriate specialties were added to the Music Department staff. Within a year—in 1969—the University Music Department was accepted with full membership in the National Association of Schools of Music. The result was outstanding performances by the students and faculty. The Arts Chorale and the Choral Society attained superior levels of excellence under the leadership of Dr. Doug

Amman and they gained international recognition after their trip to Finland.

In addition, there was the NMU Chamber Orchestra, the NMU Jazz Band, the Symphonic Wind Ensemble, the stage band, and the sports pep bands that played at basketball, football, and hockey games. The NMU marching bands performed at a number of Midwest professional football games. The department also offered a number of successful operatic offerings. The Upper Peninsula Youth Orchestra and the Upper Peninsula Select Choir provided opportunities for high school students to experience the satisfying emotion of musical performance. The Summer Youth camps attracted almost 2000 students each year to campus.

The Art and Design Department also thrived during these years. New programs of painting, sculpture, pottery and photography were added along with the necessary faculty. In 1975 the Lee Hall Art Gallery was created. The Jamrich family also supported the department with private donations.

Similar expansion and improvement was undertaken in the Drama Department. Under the direction of Dr. James Rapport, Dr. James Rasmussen, and Dr. James Panowski, the department presented a series of dramatic productions each year that attracted sell-out crowds regularly.

A popular entertainment group—considered "NMU's Entertainment Ambassadors"—was known as the Fantastics. Composed of fourteen full-time Northern students, it was formed in 1970. The Fantastics performed everything from big band to choral arrangements and comedy. Stylistically, they were all rolled up in one enthusiastic explosion of the finest in the sounds of the '50s, '60s, and '70s. The group's performance in December 1970. Within three years it had done more than 100 performances. The Fantastics performed for the USO and cut several records, which are available in the NMU Archives.

Other Areas of Expansion

The completion of the Physical Education Instructional Facility in 1976 allowed for expansion of existing programs and the introduction of new ones in all four divisions: Professional Physical Education, Required Physical Education, Health, and Recreation. Health Education and Recreation Departments saw additions of both majors and minors at the undergraduate and graduate levels. The addition of an exercise fitness laboratory with over $100,000 in equipment served to measure cardiovascular fitness and other physiological conditions. Under the supervision of area physicians, the laboratory of sports medicine served athletes, students, faculty, and the public, who are involved with the HPER community fitness program. The laboratory also made possible a community cardiac program to help in the rehabilitation of surgical patients.

For many years there was a need for a community college in Marquette, but the public refused to vote a millage for such an institution with a four-year college present. When President Jamrich arrived he moved rapidly to establish several Associate Degree programs: Associate in Science, Crafts, and Industrial Media; Media Illustration in the Department of Art and Design; and a very successful program in Criminal Justice. The School of Business added the Associate Degree to its offerings; the School of Education added Child Care Services; Aviation Technology and Medical Lab Technology offered two-year programs. Expansion in other academic areas included the introduction of programs in Anthropology and Social Work. Years before the matter became one of national significance, Northern Michigan University established a Child Development Center in 1975.

Mass communications experienced an extensive expansion in quality and programs. The programs in Mass Communications and Broadcasting were established with students working in the new facilities for WNMU-TV and WNMU-FM as well as in local radio and TV stations. With the assistance of Congressman Phil Ruppe, Northern obtained significant funding to transform WNMU-TV into a full-fledged television broadcasting facility, with a tower and cameras and related up-to-date equipment. The new facilities allowed Northern to broadcast across most of the Upper Peninsula, thus providing prospective students with insights into the University.

Off-Campus Programs

The off-campus programs allowed Northern's extension office to cover many communities throughout the Upper Peninsula, Wisconsin, and the northern Lower Peninsula. The extension center served Gogebic Community College in Ironwood, Bay de Noc Community College in Escanaba and Northwestern Michigan College in Traverse City. The three largest programs were located at K. I. Sawyer Air Force Base, Iron-Mountain, and Marquette Branch Prison. The program at K. I. Sawyer began in 1959 and over the years grew and prospered. In the fall of 1982, 434 students were enrolled in some 90 classes. During the course of its existence, more than 22,000 students had taken advantage of this service, which offered undergraduate and graduate courses. The program was well-developed: it not only offered classes but the extension office helped with academic advisement and evaluation of transcripts. It also offered advice on admissions, financial aids, academic degree programs, course scheduling, veterans' benefits, testing and registration. This service fit into President Jamrich's philosophy of extending Northern to the surrounding communities where students could easily work on their degrees while living and working at home.

Military Science

In the early 1970s—at the height of the Vietnam War and the accompanying protests nationwide and on campus—Northern launched a successful Army ROTC (Reserve Officer Training Corps) program. At first there were frequent demonstrations at President Jamrich's office against this idea, but eventually that subsided. ROTC has functioned as a successful academic/military preparation for students with that interest. The Department of the Army's Decoration for Distinguished Civilian Service was presented to President Jamrich in recognition of NMU's establishment of the successful, ROTC program even during the difficult, Vietnam era.

Women and Minorities

Even before the federal government exerted its influence in equality for women, Northern established the Women's Center for Continuing Education in 1972. The Women's Center, as it became known was opened on December 11, 1973. For the first seven years, the Center was affiliated with Northern under Continuing Education. In September 1977, the Center received a grant to fund a halfway house for women with alcohol and drug abuse problems. Through the Center a variety of workshops and research activities were launched. And in the athletic area Northern took steps to expand sports for women under Title 9.

Attention was also focused on the needs of minority students, veterans, and physically challenged students. The University answered these needs and took steps to assure students in these groups of effective support programs.

Black Student Services grew with firm administrative support. From an initial interest in Black Studies, the program expanded under the Dean of Students office with personalized services, educational and vocational counseling, group advisement, recruitment, and social activities. Under the leadership of director Harry B. Matthews and his predecessors, the program developed toward greater cultural interests. Black Culture Week became an established annual event, with noted guest speakers and nationally recognized stars of the entertainment world. The Black Student Union functioned as a day study area and a central gathering place for evening meetings or leisure hour gatherings.

The American Indian Program, initiated in Dr. Jamrich's early tenure represented a commitment in partnership between Northern Michigan University and the American Indian community of the Upper Peninsula and beyond. The administration established funding for the *Nishnawbe News*, published by the Native students and widely distributed throughout the Upper Peninsula and Canada. At some of the U. P. Tribal Centers, the University offered special courses such as Office Occupations Training and Basic Management Skills in the Keweenaw area.

A very significant event took place on the Northern campus in 1975 when the North American Indian Women's Association selected the University as the site for its annual meeting. The University also sponsored an American Indian Career Day that brought almost 300 American Indian junior and senior high school students to campus. In August 1979, Beatrice Medicine, the noted American Indian anthropologist and scholar was the commencement speaker and was awarded an honorary degree as Doctor of Humane Letters. In the early 1970s NMU introduced new courses dealing with American Indian history, one of the first in the state of Michigan, and archaeology focused on Native sites in the Upper Peninsula.

Lynn Norell, limited by a mobility handicap, desired to attend Northern like her siblings. Northern Michigan University responded to that student's motivation and point of view with special initiatives to provide access to university classrooms and other facilities beginning in 1974.

John X. Jamrich and the Board of Trustees

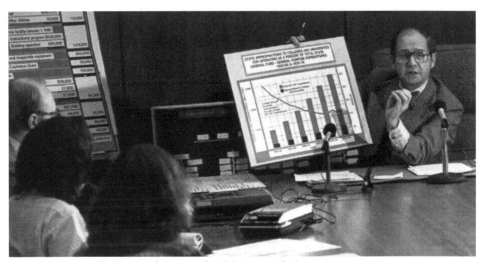

President Jamrich was famous for his use of charts

Jacobetti Complex Groundbreaking. From the left are Catherine Wright, Governor William Milliken, State Senator Joe Mack, State Representative Dominic Jacobetti, and John X. Jamrich.

President Jamrich meeting with students

J.X.J frequently took meals with students

J.X.J. on the ice

J.X.J. supporting a student cause

President Jamrich meeting with local elementary students

Former President Gerald Ford and J.X.J. (November 1978)

The Jamrich Family

June and John at home

CHAPTER 7: FACULTY, RESEARCH & AAUP

During the first fifty years of Northern's existence, there were few Ph.D.s on the faculty or even among the presidents. The first president with a doctorate was President Henry Tape, who arrived in 1940. Mildred K. Magers who taught in the English Department was the first female faculty member at Northern to receive a doctorate and that was in 1944. This was true among all of American colleges and universities at the time, so it was not much of a concern then.

The most important ingredient of a university community is the faculty. As previously described, President Harden brought up enrollment by creating a whole collection of residence halls during the 1960s. This brought in a large number of students. When Dr. Harden arrived in the fall of 1956 there were 1,090 students. Then the numbers increased by at least 100 annually in the coming years. With this increased enrollment came a demand for faculty and there were few concerns about degrees. In the fall of 1969 at the onset of the Jamrich years, a count of faculty shows that there were twenty-one with bachelor's degrees, and many fresh from the Northern classroom. The largest number of faculty—298 (56 percent)—had a master's degree while 227 (43 percent) had Ph.D.s or terminal degrees in their field.[30] There were many faculty members who "dropped in" on Northern for a year or two while they worked on their dissertation, received the Ph.D. and then moved to a larger school. During the 1960s the faculty was very unstable and transient at a time when there was a demand for faculty through the nation as colleges and universities expanded overnight. In the late 1960s it was not uncommon for a faculty member in History, for instance, to get as many as five positive job offers from around the country.

As conditions changed and the University could demand higher degrees among faculty, President Jamrich saw that faculty would plan to stay and become a long-term part of the Northern community. A stable and well-trained faculty would focus both on teaching and researching, and bring their new knowledge to the students in the classroom. Entering the Jamrich years, faculty tenure radically changed and an educator was lucky to get one job offer. As a result, the university could require the terminal degree. By 1982 a new faculty picture had emerged with 227 (68 percent) faculty having a terminal and 107 (32 percent) with a master's degree.[31]

Most of the faculty, fresh from graduate school, planned to make Northern Michigan University their home. As a result the administration sought to expand and further develop research opportunities. The opening of the Lydia Olson Library in the Edgar L. Harden Resources Center in 1967 fit perfectly into developing a research center for faculty. Ground breaking for the $5.5 million Learning Resources Center took place on June 14, 1967 and the building was opened for use in the fall of 1969. Suddenly the faculty and students had access to a growing number of books and journals: there were funds for these purchases and the library now had room for over 300,000 books. It also had an efficient inter-library loan service that provided faculty with a broad selection of books. Highly priced science journals were purchased as were collections or republished or microfilmed documents and materials. All a faculty member had to do was submit a request and it was usually acted upon. It must be remembered that this was in the age before the internet provided a connection to the wider world of knowledge. For the researcher and writer it was a golden interlude.

During the same period, Northern's periodical budget tripled from $42,000 to $123,000 annually. Unfortunately, the cost of subscriptions quadrupled, resulting in a 12 percent decrease in the number of magazines, journals, and newspapers received. However, the university's holdings in government documents tripled, while the count on audio-visual items and microfilm went up ten-fold during the previous decade.

The library's metamorphosis during the Jamrich years involved more than simple growth in the quantity of materials available. Numerous special additions improved the quality of the collection and the study environment, too. For instance in the fall of 1980 an important collection of books on Finnish-American studies was acquired from Dr. John Kolehmainen to augment Northern's holding in that area. At about the same time, the documents section of the library opened, greatly improving the availability of materials sent to it as an official U.S. government depository. The library collection has continued to grow and reshape itself in the electronic age, but not at the rate that took place during the Jamrich administration.

Since Dr. Jamrich sought to make Northern Michigan University an institution of merit, funds were set aside for research.[32] Although funds had been available earlier, faculty interest in research projects was limited. In 1964 only three faculty members sought research funds through the University. By 1972 the Academic Senate had created Faculty Research

Grants for full-time faculty to "encourage continuing intellectual growth within their chosen disciplines." Once the American Association of University Professors (AAUP) was established at NMU in 1975, faculty research became part of the contract. Besides the faculty research grants there was the Peter White Fund, established in 1964 and available for serious scholarship.

A review of the faculty research files shows that interest in research cut across the University with faculty from many departments submitting applications. By the 1970s the demand was so great that usually grants were limited to about ten annually. For instance in 1979, there were twenty-two applications for grant funding amounting to $84,205, but only $30,000 available. Other faculty and staff sought outside funding for a variety of projects, especially for those in education or dealing with university-community projects. Northern was actively interacting with the surrounding area. Many faculty members used their sabbaticals to combine research funds with the released time to pursue project both at home and abroad.

For some faculty the Northern Michigan University Press provided a ready outlet for their publications. Many of these works dealt with topics related to the Upper Peninsula and thus promoted the region. During the Jamrich years the Press published nineteen works or 58 present of the total published since the inception of the press in 1962.

A number of faculty members quickly rose to the surface as outstanding scholars who flourished in their fields of study during the Jamrich years. Dr. Fillmore C.F. Earney became an authority on marine mineral resources and mining in a number of books published during these years. Dr. Phillip Watts, who came to Northern because of the fine facilities at PEIF, went on to become noted for physiology of rock climbing, exercise physiology, biomechanics, and sports nutrition. John Hubbard received numerous faculty research grants to pursue his studies in art while others like Dr. Donald Dreisbach focused on philosophical questions. From the English Department came a number of successful researchers. Dr. Stewart Kingsbury used computers to develop a concordance for the American Dialect Society's *Dictionary of Proverbs* and Dr. Zacharias Thundyl had numerous projects going on at the same time dealing with language and religion from his native India. It is difficult to find a discipline whose faculty members were not engrossed in some type of research and writing.

Faculty members also now focused their research on the Upper Peninsula. Dr. Marla Buckmaster quickly achieved success and acclaim in her field of anthropology and archaeology for the work she did on Native American sites in northern Michigan and the Upper Peninsula. Others focused on the Finnish ethnic heritage of the region. In 1974, Finnish Culture Week was celebrated. At the same time Professor Jon Saari introduced a new course, "The Finnish Immigrant in America," which he taught until his retirement. Finnish language courses were introduced in an on-demand basis. In 1976, two sociology professors, Dr. Dale Spady and Dr. Kendrick Thompson, developed a plan for the creation of the Institute for Finnish American Studies supported by numerous Finnish-American faculty members and President Jamrich. The institute was created on February 3, 1977 and placed under the provost's office. However it was short-lived. On January 12, 1978 the Board of Trustees dissolved the institute at the request of administrators at Finlandia University in Hancock. However this interest in Finnish heritage was picked up by Dr. Michael Loukinen, a sociology professor who became interested first in his own heritage and eventually researched, wrote and directed four major documentary films. *Finnish American Lives* (1982) and *Tradition Bearers* (1983) were produced during the Jamrich tenure. It is interesting to note that when Loukinen's films were premiered the event included an interview with him and President Jamrich that was moderated by Carl Pellonpaa. In recognition of Dr. Jamrich's emphasis in establishing Northern's academic attention on Finnish heritage he was awarded the Order of the Lion of Finand. The presentation was made by ambassador, Leo Touminen followed by a formal dinner in the Finnish embassy in Washington, in December 1975.

In the field of regional history, Dr. Russell M. Magnaghi began to develop an interest and then a course on the Upper Peninsula, which ultimately led to his total involvement in the history of the region. Dr. William Robinson, professor of biology, studied the spruce grouse, loons and wolves, iconic denizens of the North Country. There were many more individual faculty members—too numerous to list—who did well during these years.

NMU also had a boat. The *Spruce Hill* was a 50-foot twin engine diesel yacht donated to the University by John McGoff in April 1977. The plan was to use the boat for Lake Superior research by University biologists and chemists. In August 1978 a major underwater research project was conducted involving a shipwreck study off Isle Royale.

Unfortunately, the boat proved impractical and the Board of Trustees authorized its sale, with the proceeds used for Lake Superior research. All of these plans, grant funding, and other faculty activities in the research world enriched their work and careers, brought their work into the classroom setting, and in a number of cases placed their documented research in the University Archives. During the Jamrich years, faculty research gained an important foothold at Northern Michigan University and continues as an important part of academic life where faculty research makes them noted authorities in their fields.

Coming of the AAUP

One of the divisive aspects of the Jamrich administration in some individuals' view was the designation of the American Association of University Professors (AAUP) as bargaining agent for the faculty. Somehow this is perceived as a failure of the administration. However it is important to study some of the background of this movement toward unionization on a national level. The development of collective bargaining at Northern was actually part of a national trend beginning in the early 1970s. At that time, local AAUP chapters began pursuing faculty collective bargaining as a means to protect professional standards and improve the economic status of faculty. This also involved its commitment to protecting academic freedom and shared governance.

Prior to the movement toward collective bargaining, the Jamrich administration had begun to get the faculty involved in University affairs. In the early years of the Jamrich administration the faculty noticed a number of initiatives that seemed to confirm the new president's commitment to greater inclusion and openness. New policies and procedures included faculty and there seemed to be new institutional power relationships on campus. One of President Jamrich's first important acts was the formation of the Task Force on Academic Governance composed of eight faculty, one student, and the vice president of Academic Affairs. Their report issued in 1969 called for a reconstituted academic senate and a new constitution, by-laws, and committee structure. As NMU Archivist Marcus Robyns noted, "The Task Force clearly intended for the new and improved Academic Senate to have a direct role in academic governance" and "envisioned a process by which the members of the university community responsibly collaborated to establish and implement the educational and administrative policies that determined the role and functions of the institution. To that end the Task

Force gave the Senate sweeping powers to control the undergraduate and graduate curriculum, advise the administration on budget and planning matters, oversee cases of dismissal, evaluation, and provide for department and school organization."[33] By August 15, 1970 the Board of Trustees voted to accept the American Association of University Professors 1966 *Statement on the Government of Colleges and Universities*, to be used to guide future decisions on university affairs. Plans moved forward and the future looked favorable for the grievance procedure followed by a retrenchment policy. The Faculty Affairs Committee developed the policy in November 1972 and President Jamrich approved it in January 1973. Jamrich wrote to Dr. Donald Heikkinen, chair of the FAC, concluding that "the expanded involvement of faculty in this produced a much better set of decisions and carried along with it some very beneficial results."

By the early 1970s Dr. Donald Heikkinen, professor in the Mathematics department, found that because of Jamrich's efforts the department, which had been very traditional, began planning, forming a number of committees, and developing a new academic government structure in the department. The faculty established advisory committees and bylaws. These bylaws served as a model through the College of Arts and Sciences and even in other colleges and universities. Smaller departments served as committees of the whole. Then Heikkinen became chairman of the Faculty Affairs Committee and they undertook to rewrite the so-called "nepotism law," and to create a maternity leave policy. This latter policy was eventually passed by the Academic Senate. Other policies developed and subsequently became part of the AAUP contract. In 1973 they also wrote a retrenchment policy that had to be used. When Dr. Heikkinen was chairman of the Academic Senate it undertook to rewrite the entire administrative practice manual. An ad hoc committee chaired by Thomas Griffith, former dean of Arts and Sciences, rewrote the manual, which was passed by the Board of Trustees. Heikkinen was asked to chair a small group of faculty and administrators to write a grievance policy which the Board approved in late 1973. Later Heikkinen discovered that this policy was used as a model discussed at national meetings. This was the precursor to the grievance procedure that also became part of the bargaining contract of AAUP.[34]

During the height of the McClellan Controversy the first attempt was made to try to unionize the faculty using the "tumultuous and angry climate on campus." By May 1968, the Michigan Educational Association (MEA) had received enough of the required request cards from the faculty to petition the Michigan Employment Relations Commission (MERC) for a collective bargaining election. When President Jamrich was notified of this action he personally met with the organizers and asked them to postpone their action so he would have time in the coming year to present his program for improvements of shared governance and address other issues of concern to the faculty. The MEA agreed to give Jamrich a chance and called off their organizing effort.

During these developments an unfortunate case developed in 1971 over the termination of a faculty member due to a lack of a Ph.D. and poor teaching. The faculty felt that this was a violation of due process. The Faculty Review Panel took up the case and after lengthy hearings supported the faculty member. President Jamrich rejected the Panel's recommendations and upheld the termination. This action incensed many faculty members including Dr. Robert McClellan who concluded that "the faculty member at Northern Michigan University served at the pleasure of the administration, period." Obviously he remembered as other faculty did, his own struggle with the administration over termination.

The second event that annoyed many faculty members, who saw themselves as increasingly irrelevant, was the promotion of Dr. Robert Glenn as the new provost and vice president for Academic Affairs. Despite the fact that the Selection Advisory Committee did not put Glenn among the top three candidates for the position, President Jamrich selected him, concluding that as dean, Glenn had proven his "ability to approach complicated problems analytically and personnel problems with a deep human concern." Many faculty, some of whom did not like Glenn's bluntness and autocratic style, were outraged by this action and saw it as more proof of the administration's disregard of the faculty.

A third important element came from off-campus and involved Michigan's economic misfortunes at the time. A reduced allocation from the state seemed to necessitate lay-offs. This "compounded the faculty's feelings of helplessness and vulnerability and exacerbated the tensions with the administration. Many faculty felt that 'creeping retrenchment' was underway and they had no control over the outcome." Younger faculty cautiously watched the outcome, but without a plan of action except to seek a new position elsewhere if they were on the lower end of the hiring ladder.

The other development in the years prior to 1975 was the struggle among the Michigan Education Association, the American Association of University Professors, and the Northern administration over the unionization of the faculty and collective bargaining. It was a complicated tale of a variety of personalities, varying agendas, and conflicting philosophies. President Jamrich saw this development as the creation of an "industrial union model" that was out of place in a university environment. Throughout ths attempt to get a union on campus, Dr. Jamrich naturally fought to keep unionization out. The long and complicated episode can be best reviewed in Marcus C. Robyns and Carrie Fries's booklet, *Blood on the Table.*[35] Finally in May 1975, the AAUP was successfully established on campus in a vote by the faculty. Dr. Jamrich has left us with his memories of the union election, "It was not a 'battle' by any criteria, but was a vigorous exercise of the democratic process via election; that was my approach to the issue." He continued, "After the MEA vs AAUP voting, and more than one 'yes-no' vote, the final vote is one I clearly respected."[36]

This does not end the story: now the administration and the AAUP Bargaining Council had to sit down, negotiate and craft a union contract. At first there was a rather violent verbal struggle between the AAUP chief negotiator Dr. Robert McClellan, and the administration negotiator, James Tobin, the university attorney. The teams had previous policy developments by the faculty and university to work from as they held their negotiations. However when an impasse developed in April 1976, the AAUP team authorized Dr. James Greene, who had been involved with the process, to quietly approach President Jamrich with the goal of breaking the impasse. This was accomplished in rather typical Jamrich fashion. After reading over the proposal that Green had earlier delivered and digesting it, Dr. Jamrich invited Greene to his residence and after a lengthy discussion the president agreed to intervene with the administration's negotiating team. On the following day, May 3, 1976, Dr. Jon Saari, the new AAUP negotiator, announced that an agreement had been reached. Thus ended years of rancor and anger over the coming of AAUP to campus. From the available evidence it seems that the Board of Trustees took a hard line with the advent of the union, which ultimately made President Jamrich look bad to the faculty, but that story remains for others to pursue.

CHAPTER 8: SPORTS AND ATHLETICS

President Jamrich was influenced by his former mentor and co-worker President John A. Hannah of Michigan State University. President Hannah espoused a strong athletic program—along with music, theater, debate and other extra-curricular programs—to showcase the university. The 15 years of the Jamrich administration thus became a period of unprecedented growth and success in intercollegiate athletics. Ranking at the head of athletic accomplishments since the mid-1960s was the establishment of ice hockey at the Division I level of competition, the initiation of a variety of programs for women, and the national exposure the university received with its many successful NCAA post-session appearances.

"Dr. Jamrich was very instrumental in the growth of our total athletic program," reported NMU athletic director Gildo Canale. "He had a great influence in the formation of the Mid-Continent Conference, which allowed many of our athletes to compete against the best Division II competition available."

"He recognized the importance of ice hockey to the community, was greatly influential in the growth of the women's program, and was always sympathetic to our needs with his continual support in tough economic times."

"I think that was evident with his recognition of the potential of the Golden Wildcat Club and his encouragement to this organization to participate in providing financial support".

Northern had already made the move from the NAIA to the NCAA prior to Dr. Jamrich's arrival on campus in 1968, but it was several years before the university began reaping the rewards of NCAA post-season play.

Athletes from individual qualification sports such as gymnastics, skiing, swimming, and wrestling began making regular NCAA appearances during Jamrich's tenure and in 1973 two of them—wrestler Gil Damiani and Nordic skier Pertti Reijula—won individual national championship titles.

In 1975 the Wildcat football squad became the first to qualify for NCAA post-season play in a team-only sport and promptly won the Division II national championship. It was the first of six post-season playoffs in the next eight years for the girders, who reached the semifinals on two occasions and were quarterfinalists the other three times.

Basketball put together a string of three consecutive post-season appearances beginning in 1979 and twice reached the quarterfinal round after winning Division II regional playoff titles. And hockey, which did not exist as a varsity sport prior to the 1976-77 season, reached the NCAA's Final Four in Division I in 1980-81 after winning Central Collegiate Hockey Association regular season and playoff titles. The Wildcats were national runners-up in 1980 and finished fourth in the following year.

A little known and all-but-forgotten sport of championship caliber was bowling. The sport was first promoted in the late 1950s by Dr. Rico Zenti for faculty and students. The teams "rolled" at local alleys until 1966 when the on-campus alley was built in the University Center. Over the years, students won a number of awards for their skill. Northern's bowling team led by Mike Bauman won the 1969 National College Team Championship held in Chicago by amassing a score of 7,683 topping the University of Tennessee.[37]

The late 1960s saw the inception of Northern's varsity program for women after the rationale for such a move was approved by the University Board of Trustees on Dr. Jamrich's recommendation. Northern's first all-female athletic team competed in field hockey in 1968, basketball was added in 1970-71, Nordic and downhill skiing in 1971-72, volleyball in 1974, gymnastics and swimming in 1977-78, and tennis in 1978. Downhill skiing and tennis were subsequently dropped in the early 2000s because of financial considerations. Women athletes won individual national championships in skiing and swimming. The first was freshman Francine Malindzak who was the 1979 AIAW slalom and alpine combined national ski champion. The first NCAA female national champion was diver Jodi Stout who captured the Division II one-meter crown in 1983. Women's teams won state championships in basketball and volleyball, state and regional titles in field hockey and competed at the national level in skiing, gymnastics, swimming and field hockey.

"Dr. Jamrich was very, very supportive of and sensitive to the development of the women's program," stated retired NMU associate athletic director Barb Patrick, who was responsible for women's intercollegiate athletics. "He allowed us to develop and direct our own programs."

The major addition to the men's program during the Jamrich administration was the establishment of men's ice hockey at the Division I level during the 1976-77 season. Long popular in a community that supports an extensive junior hockey program, competition at the college level was an instant success. Wildcat teams played in front of standing-room-only crowds at the city owned Lakeview Arena, and within four years qualified for the NCAA playoffs, and as mentioned, finished as national runner-up in 1980.

Jamrich, who made his final appearance at an NMU athletic function when he delivered remarks at the 1983 annual spring sports award banquet, took a great deal of pride in the success of Northern's teams and individual athletes.

CHAPTER 9: BRICKS AND MORTAR

<u>Construction</u>

At the beginning of his tenure at NMU, from abstract notions of transparency and shared governance, Jamrich quickly turned to some practicalities. With the development of new programs and majors and the movement to attract more students and serve the people of the Upper Peninsula and Michigan, came a demand for construction of new facilities for the expansion. The state of Michigan had to appropriate monies for these construction projects and thus the good offices of State Representative Dominic Jacobetti and State Senator Joe Mack were essential to the process. Dr. Jamrich's past experience and his analytical mind and training in mathematics served him well in his presentations to the Legislature of Northern's operational and capital outlay needs. As Miriam Hilton pointed out, "He applied systematic data analysis procedures to set forth Northern's needs in charts and diagrams which convinced the most skeptical legislators that he thoroughly understood the institution he was employed to administer. As a result of his efforts, the per capita state appropriation to Northern for operating funds increased by nearly 50 percent from 1968 to 1973."

As David McClintock, building coordinator of the campus plan, pointed out, all of the construction that went on during the Jamrich administration stemmed from the many residence halls built by President Harden. As the enrollment increased, students needed more classroom, lab and library space, so the accumulation of bricks and mortar snowballed.[38]

The Harden administration asked for funds to renovate the original buildings—Kaye, Longyear, and Peter White halls. McClintock attended the meetings with capital outlay people in the state legislature. The discussions continued and then the state fire marshal condemned Kaye Hall, scotching any possibility for Northern to get state funding for a renovation project. The state would and did fund the Edgar L. Harden Learning Resources Center, but demanded that it be larger than requested so Northern would not run out of space in a few years.

Ground breaking for the $5.5 million Learning Resources Center took place on June 14, 1967 and the building was completed in February 1969 and opened for use in the fall. The top two floors housed the Lydia M. Olson Library, which has a 300,000 book capacity. The first floor had space for 220 faculty offices. On the lower level are offices and broadcasting space for WMNU-TV and WNMU-FM. The opening of this building was a milestone for the University and met a need for more and efficient space.

The second important building in the new campus complex was the construction of the Instructional Facility, which began in the summer of 1968 and was completed in the spring of 1970 at a cost of $2.7 million. Covering 97,850 square feet, it originally contained 28 classrooms and two learning laboratories on the second floor. On the first floor, was a 500-seat lecture hall and four smaller lecture halls. A basement level had faculty offices and storage rooms.

Originally it was called IF for Instructional Facility. Then on October 17, 1975, the Board of Trustees acted on a motion offered by Dr. Fred Sabin of Marquette who said the motion "reflected the Board's strong feel for the superb job Dr. Jamrich has done for NMU." It was passed unanimously and dedication took place in December. At the time, many people were critical of this move—naming the hall after a living president. However as time has passed and the Jamrich administration is carefully reviewed and scrutinized, it seems an appropriate move.

The first Jamrich Hall remained in use until the end of the 2014 winter semester. During that summer the building was demolished, having been replaced by the new Jamrich Hall. For many alumni and faculty it was a bittersweet demolition to watch.

The completion of old Jamrich Hall and the Edgar L. Harden Learning Resources Center in 1969 created a quadrangle, the Academic Mall. The Mall facilitated travel especially by the students from their dorms to classrooms and around the campus. This gave the campus a new sense of unity.

By the early 1970s there was little use made of Kaye Hall as most activity had moved to the other side of the campus. Since the state legislature would not fund renovation of any unsafe original building, a new administration building was anticipated. When word came out that the campus icon, beloved Kaye Hall, would be demolished, there was controversy among the community and alumni. Even David McClintock was sorry to see the loss of a building he had grown up with. The controversy boiled for months and, as McClintock stated, instead of the administration acting on criticism, it reacted to it and he felt that a different approach could have been taken. Kaye Hall, the Peter White Hall of Science and the Olson Library were demolished while as a compromise Longyear Hall was left standing for future disposition.

Construction of the six-story Cohodas Hall began in October 1973 and work was completed by late July 1975. Most administrative offices were located in the building. Data processing originally occupied the basement. The main floor housed business offices, central receiving, information, and a campus monitoring system. The rest of the five floors were devoted to administrative offices and meeting space and related activities. So by this time the basic "new" campus had been created to deal with the expanded enrollment.

In an attempt to commemorate lost Kaye Hall with its beautiful sandstone walls, a new structure arose on campus. Original sandstone was recycled when Board of Trustees member and Panax Corporation President John P. McGoff donated $40,000 for a pair of carillon towers on campus.

In the fall of 1972, Nell Sprinkle donated to NMU a 12-inch reflecting telescope (12-inch, F; 6 Newtonian telescope with a precision equatorial drive), the mirror on it hand-crafted by her husband Lloyd. In 1974, NMU purchased the dome that encompasses the entire telescope and a year later the Sprinkle Observatory was in use. Located on the roof of the New Science Center, the observatory is used by students in astronomy classes, visited by middle and high school students, and is occasionally used by the public. This little known addition to the campus extends the teaching capability of Physics professors.

The athletic program, begun with football in 1904, slowly developed over the years. In 1958 Hedgcock Field House was opened to replace extremely crowded and totally inadequate facilities in Kaye Hall. Once again the expanded enrollment and the development of the athletic program in the Jamrich years demanded a larger facility—the PEIF or Physical Education Instructional Facility. Groundbreaking was held on October 19, 1974. The sprawling structure cost $9.9 million, over a million dollars above the original cost. The building housed a number of specialized features and equipment that physical education instructors felt were sorely needed at Northern. Among these was the "Instructional Ice Arena," the first completed section of the building, which was opened at a public ceremony on September 19, 1976. Although the newly created hockey team only used the ice sheet for practice, it had a series of carpeted locker rooms and a warming room for public skaters. In order to promote skating among the students, the Health, Physical Education and Recreation Department ordered 250 pair of skates.

The building was completed in mid-October 1976 and opened for intramural and recreational use. The building was an immediate success and well-used by students and the community. It was a major improvement over the earlier facilities, so advanced that Dr. Phil Watts, when seeking to settle into a permanent position, decided on Northern due to the facility. He went on to become a world-expert and author on rock climbing.

The last major structure built in the Jamrich years was the Jacobetti Complex. An important component to the local community in Alger and Marquette counties was the development of Northern's community college focus. It should be remembered that only twenty-five percent of high school students go on to college. The Jacobetti Complex provides training for the many seeking non-academic careers. The Complex got its start as a seven-building school scattered throughout Marquette dating back to 1962 with President Kennedy's Manpower Development and Training Act. The goal of this legislation was to retrain people who had lost their jobs or who were without skills for industry.

The Area Training Center evolved into the NMU Skills Center, which offered classes not only to those pursuing a post-secondary degree, but to high school students interested in vocational training and entry to well-paying jobs. During the Jamrich administration it became obvious that all of these sites had to be located under one roof. State Representative Dominic Jacobetti, was extremely interested in the situation that would benefit his constituents and worked with the administration to develop plans for what would become the Jacobetti Complex in 1977. Soon construction began on a $16.5 million facility at the north end of campus. The building, covering five acres and 225,000 square feet under one roof, opened in 1980. The Complex served people of varying abilities sixteen years of age and over. Today it has merged with a variety of programs—culinary arts, hospitality management, cosmetology, automotive repair, aviation maintenance, construction management, building technology, electronics, engineering, industrial technology, plastics injection and other skilled trades.

The first campus presidential residence opened to President Henry and Mrs. Tape in 1954, located on Kaye Avenue across from the University Center. Over the years it went through various renovations, but due to the expansion of Marquette General Hospital the property was sold and a new home was constructed on Center Street. The Board of Trustees named the new residence after President James Kaye and in 1980 the Jamrichs moved in.

One project attempted but not realized during the Jamrich years was the All Events Center. The idea for such a structure went back to 1969 with discussions to create a structure that would include an indoor football field and an area that could be used for convocations and conferences by both the university and the community. The project kept going up the list of state financial appropriations. In 1971-1972 there was a plan to take a student vote whereby students would add $20 per semester to their fees for the construction of such a building. If so, there would be no need for a state appropriation. If the University had received the student pledge construction would have gone ahead but this did not occur.[39]

With talk of an Olympic Training Center coming to campus the name of the proposed structure changed to a Sports Training Complex and eventually led to the Superior Dome, which opened years later in 1991.

Campus Plan

In 1973, Johnson, Johnson and Roy, Inc. prepared a plan for the physical development of the University. The plan, funded by appropriations from the State Legislature, established flexible guidelines for the orderly physical growth of the campus in an imaginative design. Consideration were made for the severe winter climate, building height, and open space percentage. The plan called for a growth pattern offering new access routes from the west, with the traditional entrance on Presque Isle Avenue probably to remain the same. Dr. Jamrich negotiated the purchase of the triangle of land from the Cliffs Dow Charcoal Company. Recommendations were made for securing additional land to the north with a projected campus size of 345 acres by 1980. Northern has followed the plan outline: on-campus acreage between 1970 and 1980 rose from 217 to 323, only 22 acres short of the 1980 goal and with the addition of Cohodas Hall, Jamrich Hall, Harden Learning Resources Center, and Jacobetti Complex, campus buildings totaled nearly 2,500,000 square feet.

Besides these major structure improvements to meet the modern demands of the students and faculty on campus, there were a number of minor land changes. In the 1970s Northern obtained the triangle of land bound by Lakeshore, Fair and Pine Streets. Then in return for the old Palestra (former ice hockey rink) property, Dr. Jamrich saw to it as a good community leader that ten acres were given to the city of Marquette for the construction of the ever-popular Lakeview Arena and the site for

Northern hockey games for many of the team's early years. The land bordering Lake Superior provided Northern with a little-known beach, that students and President Jamrich hoped to develop into a recognized campus park.[40]

CHAPTER 10: STUDENTS AND ALUMNI

Admissions Office

Enrollment concerns were on the mind of President Jamrich from the beginning.[41] During the previous Harden administration the focus for enrollment was the right-to-try philosophy, and there was less concern to attract high quality high school students. Large numbers of students came to Northern but many of them were high risk, quickly failed, and left.

In the summer of 1973, President Jamrich noted that there were "serious challenges before us in the field of admissions." He declared that "college enrollments are reaching a plateau and may well decline in the next several years. To meet this challenge we at Northern must undertake vigorous and imaginative new programs to attract students to this quality institution." He stressed that Northern's admissions program not only sought to recruit students, but it must aim to provide a broad range of services to high school counselors, students and parents seeking to pursue some kind of education beyond the high school diploma.[42]

President Jamrich wanted higher caliber students. He felt that if NMU attracted a class valedictorian then other students would follow and the number of quality students would rise. Although enrollments were increasing and he was proud of the work done by the Admissions Office, he was also concerned that at some future date enrollments might decline and plans should be developed to meet such a decline.

As a result, intricate plans were developed. At first Alumni Ambassadors were organized to meet with students in respective communities and set plans for the arrival of admissions people. Later admissions people went into the field to meet with students and promote Northern. Finally by the mid-1970s, centers were opened in Detroit, Lansing, and Kalamazoo to work with students. In the Upper Peninsula, NMU admissions people visited two and three times a year to work with high school counselors who had gone to Northern to promote their alma mater. The Chicago area also had an admissions officer who worked the northern suburbs. In order to attract better students NMU offered financial incentives of $2,000 scholarship for National Merit Scholarship finalists. The pre-med and pre-law programs were very attractive to many students and developed excellent reputations of getting graduates into medical and law schools. Monies for these scholarships came from state, federal and private sources and were readily available for the Admissions Office. At one point President Jamrich met with Jack Kunkel, director of admissions, and told him that the resources—scholarships and travel monies—were available for recruitment and all he had to do was implement a plan and work on recruitment. However Jamrich noted that Kunkel would be directly accountable. This approach appealed to Kunkel and his staff. The results were outstanding and met President Jamrich's goal for on-going increases in enrollment.

Enrollment

In the first decades of the twentieth-first century the problem with student enrollments is critical for Northern and colleges and universities throughout the United States. Back in the 1960s this was not the case. During President Harden's first year (1956-1957) the student body numbered around 1,200 students and by the time he left in 1967 there were over 7,000 students. This trend throughout the nation was not restricted to Northern. Thus at the opening of the Jamrich administration (1968) there were 7,286 students and this number grew to 9,548 in 1975-76, an all-time high. This increase in enrollment was due to the work of the Admissions Office and exposure through WNMU-TV and WNMU-FM. During the Jamrich tenure, there were over 20,000 graduates of Northern. That was more than the total of all graduates up to 1968.

The university was nearly overwhelmed by the growing number of students on campus. Housing and dining facilities were crowded, classes were full, and faculty and staff were stressed over trying to find classes and spaces for the growing number of arriving students. As dire as this seemed to some people, it was a positive development. As we have seen President Jamrich was always concerned about enrollments. He noted in the fall of 1973 that as he looked at the figures there was a national trend of decreasing enrollments in institutions of higher education that he said "underscores the efforts of our admissions staff, faculty, and others put forth in attracting new students to campus. These efforts insure the continued strength of Northern in its drive to serve the higher education needs of the citizens of the Upper Peninsula and the state of Michigan."[43]

Development Fund

Raising monies for the University became increasingly important as state funding began to decline. Individuals such as Sam Cohodas and John McGoff gave sizeable donations to the University. In December 1973 Cohodas tendered a gift of $250,000, the largest to that date, toward the new hall to be named in his honor. He also endowed several scholarships and a chair of banking. John McGoff, a newspaper man and member of the Board of Trustees in 1978, gave $300,000 for the McGoff Distinguished Lecture series. His goal was to enhance the quality of life at Northern and to contribute to the development of the University as an educational and social institution of greater stature and leadership. The first distinguished speaker was former president Gerald R. Ford, who visited campus for several days in November 1978.

Gifts to the NMU Development Fund in 1981 topped the half-million dollar mark for the first time and was a 50 percent increase over the previous year. The number of persons giving—alumni and friends of Northern—had taken a dramatic upswing from 6,300 to 10,200. As the president of the Development Fund, Ellwood A. Mattson stated, "Despite adverse economic conditions, the fund has continued its rapid growth rate." He was pleased that the fund was making an impact on a number educational programs as this funding was critical and would be in the future as well. By fall 1982 the endowment fund topped a million dollars, another first in Northern's history.

In late 1977 the President's Club was established. Four years later, it totaled some 200 members, all of whom contributed at least $1,000 annually for five years. Also members made optional deferred gifts of $15,000 or more in a bequest, life insurance policy, or other testamentary instrument. Just relying on the minimum gifts, it was projected that in five years the University would reap the benefit of $870,000.

Student Guidelines

From the beginning of President Jamrich's tenure there was a concern for clearly defined rules and regulations for students and their involvement in the affairs of the University. One of the key figures in developing many of these policies was Dr. Norman Hefke.[44] He was engaged in student affairs from 1968 when he was assistant dean of students and associate dean 1969-1979. He dealt with discipline cases and developed policy, a student code, student ordinances and university ordinances and a judicial system for students. Faculty, staff and students produced a students' rights document in three years. Hefke also dealt with the distributing or sale of student publications and materials, a speaker's policy, re-entry students, and alcohol in the residence halls. This was a changing time when the University would no longer be stepping in as parent for students away from home, they would have behavior guidelines to follow.

In 1979 Hefke became dean of students. He found that Dr. Jamrich was very interested in the students and problems that they might have which could be solved by the administration. Dr. Hefke recounted that President Jamrich took a personal hands-on approach and would visit students in the residence halls, have dinner with them, listen to their problems and then contact Dr. Hefke to look into them and see what could be done to improve the quality of student life and this, their experience at Northern.[45] He also met on a regular basis with a cadre of high achieving students to get their views of life on campus and in the classroom. As Dr. Robert Archibald remembers in the early 1970s, when he was a student, President Jamrich would invite five students to have lunch with him in the University Center, and then affably had a conversation with them about their work.[46]

Student Involvement

In February 1982, the administration reported that Northern had more opportunities for student involvement in the decision-making process than at six other public colleges surveyed in the state. President Jamrich made it a point to meet with members of the Associated Students of NMU, the staff of the student newspaper *The North Wind* and residence hall councils and other similar groups. He also maintained open communications with students. Over the years Dr. Jamrich had maintained "open office" hours, that allowed students to visit with him without an appointment. NMU's chief executive had asked the students for their ideas and suggestions on tuition levels for 1982-1983, financial aid, room and board rates, Lakeview expansion plans, budget reduction plans and similar items.[47] This type of involvement was an important factor in Dr. Jamrich's role as president.

By the end of 1982, students entered a new age in registering at Northern. A pilot "on-line" computerized registration system was tried and proved highly successful, fast and efficient for students who no longer had to stand in long lines seeking class cards only to find the class closed.

Alumni Office

The Alumni Office goes back to the early days of Northern. By the 1960 there were over 20,000 alums. The Alumni Officers worked closely with President Jamrich's goals. A number of alumni from around the country but especially in Michigan and surrounding states served as Alumni Ambassadors and worked to connect with high school students to promote Northern Michigan University as their college of choice. The alumni were encouraged to make contributions to the University's scholarship programs and became an important part of the University's goal for a stellar institution.

Public Safety

With the growing number of students on campus, Northern took on the shape of a good-sized community with attendant problems. As a result, Public Safety developed. Until around 1966 it was a Security Department and then became a Police Department until 1969. At that time the name was changed to Public Safety and Bill Lyons took over. A decade later Ken Chant took over and the name was changed to Public Safety and Police Services to better reflect its full operation on the Northern campus. In the process the department became professionalized, reflecting its new expanded operation.[48]

CHAPTER 11: THE CURTAIN DROPS

John Jamrich's presidency was affected by external events and developments over which he had little control but nevertheless had to deal with. It is rather amazing that during the difficult and tumultuous times of the late 1960s and through the decade of the 1970s, while many university presidents were unable to cope with the changing situations, John Jamrich persisted at the helm and not only survived but pushed the University ahead.

Dr. Jamrich arrived at Northern Michigan University to deal with a problem not of his making, and in the early 1980s once again forces well beyond his control in the national and state economies were working to challenge his administrative and management ability. In the winter 1982 term enrollment declined by 306 students below the previous year—exactly the concern that Dr. Jamrich had a number of years earlier when the enrollments were more robust. The reasons for the decline included the federal government's cutback in financial assistance to students, a downtrodden economy, migration from Michigan to other states, and the end of a post-war baby boom.[49]

This decline was part of a worsening economy—reduced auto production and sales, a housing market at a standstill, and a resulting depression—then facing the state of Michigan. Reduction had been made to the state budget for higher education in previous years. And now by executive order from Governor William Milliken, there would be a $5 million cut for Northern during the months of July, August and September of 1982. This cut came in spite of the $5.5 million in reduced expenditures already made in the previous 33 months. In order to meet this deficit and create a balanced budget, President Jamrich explained that a calendared and prescribed series of steps would be set into place with the faculty union to identify reductions in the instructional budget and the number of faculty who might be terminated. As President Jamrich said "Northern is facing the most difficult fiscal situation in Michigan's history. It must maintain composure and confidence to deal successfully with the problems that are confronting us."

In typical Jamrich fashion, he took his ideas for fiscal savings to the Board, officers of the unions, ASNMU and others. He had proposed two alternative approaches to balancing the budget for 1982-83. Alternative A: everyone at Northern would forego salary increases totaling $2.2 million for the new fiscal year. This included the possibility of several days off without pay. Each day off without pay—if everyone participated—would yield $80,000 in savings. A $3 million deficit could be wiped out if staff and faculty declined a salary increase and took ten days off without pay. Alternative B: restructuring, consolidating, and perhaps eliminating some academic programs and University services. To achieve $3 million savings in this alternative would require program and service modifications that would result in the termination of 105 to 125 faculty and staff. However in this setting an unemployment compensation obligation of about $500,000 would confront the University. As President Jamrich put it, "I have given this matter many, many hours of thought and discussion. It is my strong recommendation that we consider Alternative A, plus some other minimal actions for the coming year as the best approach to balancing the budget." What followed in the *News-Review* of April 1982 was a detailed explanation of the options and conclusions. Faculty at the time and later, felt that Dr. Jamrich was overstating the problem and that there were other remedies. Future historians can examine this assessment, but for now it is primarily important to show the problem and how President Jamrich planned to deal with it.

The fiscal problem continued to be discussed with hopes for an agreement on a salary freeze. By the fall of 1982 a great deal of work by the administration and complicated state plans for repayment of withheld funds effected a solution. However at the same time there were faculty layoffs although, "we would have preferred the more humane approach of saving these jobs through salary concessions or some similar arrangement." Throughout this financial crunch, President Jamrich was determined to maintain a quality education at Northern.

Then President Jamrich announced his retirement shortly after having celebrated his 62th birthday on June 12th. His decision had nothing to do with the financial problems facing the state of Michigan. As he has stated, "In my case, it [financial crisis] definitely was not a factor in my retirement decision. I recall the Board discussion around the table during the first meeting I attended. The subject of length of tenure came up. I suggested the F.W. Woolworth criterion of five and/or ten; with a little laughter, there seemed to be general agreement. However, I 'overstayed' the guideline with the Board's approach."[50] With this announcement Dr. Jamrich was asked about his plans for the future and he responded that he had not had time to even think of his plans after stepping down and that he planned to concentrate on the vital work of the coming year.

As 1982 moved into 1983, Dr. Jamrich had to continue to deal with the state budget shortfall. He had to report to the Board of Trustees in December 1982, that "the surge of red ink has not yet reached flood stage." However despite these decreases, ever optimistic, Dr. Jamrich went ahead and asked for a state increase for new programs, equipment and faculty and staff salaries.

By March, President Jamrich announced that administrators including himself would take voluntary pay cuts. For each day off without pay that might be imposed for other employees, the administrators would return two days' pay to the University General Fund. Earlier in the month Jamrich stated that salary concessions from Northern employees might be necessary if the University planned to maintain the scope of academic programs and services and to minimize faculty-staff layoffs. The situation was dire and on April 1 the Board of Trustees at Jamrich's request determined that a "financial exigency" existed and authorized negotiations with the AAUP faculty union on reductions in the instructional budget. It also authorized reopening of contract discussions with Northern's other unions to achieve budget reductions through layoffs and-or wage concessions. This was the first time in Northern's 83 year history that "financial exigency" was invoked.

As early as February 1982 voluntary annualized teaching was in place so that faculty could teach their 24 credit hours throughout the year and their compensation saved especially for summer school. This was another way to survive. By this time a number of full-time temporary positions had been terminated but no tenured faculty members. Departments took action where they could to save money. The Geography Department closed its wildlife field station in 1981; Criminal Justice terminated its satellite residency at Northwestern Michigan College in Traverse City.

President Jamrich sought salary cuts from the members of the AAUP. The president of the AAUP John Kiltinen wanted to see more information on the state budget. Some people could not imagine the serious nature of this financial crisis. The AAUP responded with a nine-page paper that called for reductions in "top administrative positions and their associated high salaries." The union also suggested that a nine-month academic year appointment should be imposed for non-teaching staff and administrators as is the case for the faculty. Summer employment should be allowed only when need was demonstrated. The AAUP also suggested the elimination of the football program and moving all sports except hockey into the NCAA Division III. At the state level, the AAUP supported Governor Milliken's income tax increase as extra revenue was needed for education. These suggestions were not adopted by the administration.

However on April 1, 1983 the AAUP ratified a one-year contract, 140-51, that consisted of a withdrawal of the 19 faculty layoff notices in exchange for an average 1.87 percent reduction in base salaries and other financial sacrifices as announced by Dr. James Greene, faculty negotiator. They also planned to have a contract salary reopener for the coming 1983-84 budget. AAUP President John Kiltinen stated that the faculty had made significant contributions and adjustments to teaching summer sessions in Arts and Sciences. The latter would figure as part of a faculty's regular assignment rather than for extra pay. Through the financial crisis the faculty increased their productivity and did not slack off because of the problem. However issues of *The North Wind* show that buildings were closed, stations closed and there were cuts in graduate funding.

President Jamrich announced his retirement in early August 1982 several weeks after his 62th birthday. A large gathering of University and community folks attended the gala retirement party held on May 20, 1983 in which community leaders and others praised his very successful administration.

Despite the fiscal problems that President Jamrich faced squarely—as was his style—the entire 15 years of his administration was assessed by the Board of Trustees at their spring meeting in 1983. They were highly pleased with his service to the University and outlined the benchmarks of the Jamrich presidency: 1. Faculty with the terminal degree increased from 32 percent to 72 percent; 2. Physical plant expansion from $43 million to $87 million; 3. Major program development in Nursing, Criminal Justice, Business and Management, and Art and Design, and establishment of the Education Specialist degree and a strong pre-professional program; 4. Substantial lowering of the student-faculty ratio and quadrupling of library books to over 370,000; 5. Major advancements in student services, including programs for disadvantaged, minorities, and handicapped students; and 6. Lowest combined tuition, room and board rates and the strongest student financial aid program in Michigan. The resolution cited the President's wife, June, noting the Jamrichs have "served together as a team."

Across campus, the student viewpoint was enunciated by *The North Wind* editor Mary Boyd in an editorial titled, "Farewell Wishes to

President Jamrich." She noted that Jamrich's tenure as president was marked by many achievements and some controversy. In conclusion she stated, "Overall, President Jamrich's time with us has clearly benefited Northern Michigan University." He was one of the longest tenured presidents in the state. Then she continued "Perhaps his ability has been best shown in getting funds from state legislators and commanding their respect. This success has allowed for physical and academic development and for increased appropriations. It kept tuition and room and board among the lowest in the state and increased financial aid dollars from the university's general find. While there is much to criticize, criticism is inevitable for a person who has any kind of decision-making responsibility. The buck does stop at his desk and he must act with the university as a whole in mind. His leadership role in developing Northern's status as a competitive state university deserves commendation."[51]

CHAPTER 12: THE MAN AND THE WOMAN

The Man

John Jamrich was a multifaceted individual of whom some people only saw one dimension. As a result he receives mixed reviews in peoples' memories. He could be seen as a caring family man; a strong presidential leader whose decisions drew applause or disparagement by faculty, students, and community members; or as a key player with the Board of Trustees as they managed the University.

So, who was John X. Jamrich?

The Board of Trustees found Jamrich an exemplary leader. In his relationship with the Board he openly took the position that the president serves the wishes and plans of the Board. So the view of Board members is important in understanding the man and his presidency. Those who worked with him generally argued that he provided the University with strong personal direction and often those with whom he worked were amazed by the depth and breadth of his knowledge in their specific areas of expertise. As Northern's chief executive officer he was always sensitive to and worked effectively with the Board. As Board chairman Fred Sabin stated long ago "it was a pleasure to have him at the helm." The high regard that the Board had for him led them to name the Instructional Facility after him.

Other members of the Board found him willing to shoulder the burden with such equanimity that he never passed the buck nor blamed others for a decision he had made. He was a strong leader who from the beginning at Northern sought input from his staff and considered all of the options. But once he made a decision, he took responsibility and any consequences.

Richard Jones, Northern's chief legal counsel with Miller, Canfield, Paddock & Stone, remembered the Jamrich years: "The term of your presidency was long and highly successful by comparison to others in the 70s and 80s. I always admired the skill and devotion to the best interests of the university that were consistently evident in your work."

Being a fiscal conservative was a great help in the difficult budgetary times that occurred often during John Jamrich's administration. He had an excellent management style and was a tireless worker. He had the capacity to assimilate data and on certain issues would involve faculty, students and staff when discussing a policy or problem. Dr. Thomas Knauss noted that in the realm of athletics Jamrich worked closely with the Athletic Council when it was dealing with tough problems concerning national and conference rules, the budget, cuts, or hiring coaches. In 1981, controversial History professor Dr. Robert McClellan wrote to Jamrich, "As I discuss matters with faculty and administrators from other schools it becomes apparent that Northern has survived better than most. Much of the credit for preserving intact the essential functions of the University must go to your efforts. You have not had an easy task and I am sure that the personal strain has not been inconsiderable."[52]

His work schedule inspired many. He arrived at the office early and left late and was a very effective administrator. Using his past experience and his expertise, he strengthened existing programs and created new ones—nursing, pre-med, women's athletics, and the computer center. He improved the quality of the faculty and created a diversity of academic programs with major changes. He remained committed to faculty quality and how the university could financially support expanded research. Jamrich knew that knowledge gained in lab studies or documentary research would eventually accrue to students in the classrooms.

Personally, those who got to know John Jamrich first found him to be a Christian gentleman in the strongest sense of the word. He and June were members of Messiah Lutheran Church in Marquette and Pastor "Kal" Kalwett said that the Jamrichs took an active role in church affairs. They participated in the church's stewardship program and hosted some of the every-member-response meetings in their home.

Pastor Kalwett found him to be well-read in the Bible and theology. Jamrich also contributed his time by accepting a term on the board of trustees for Carthage College, a Lutheran institution in Kenosha, Wisconsin.

Outside of the church walls, Jamrich had a caring spirit and often helped students with funds loaned from his wallet. On other occasions, at least one I am familiar with, he intervened when a faculty member was let go by a department for lack of a degree. Needing medical insurance quickly, the faculty member found that Dr. Jamrich got him a permanent position in an administrative office in the University. It is rare for university presidents to take such action. Even during the perilous times of "financial exigency" of 1982, Dr. Jamrich was concerned with taking a more humane approach in these terms. These acts of kindness and thoughtfulness are part of his DNA.

Another important trait is his strong sense of history. Dr. Jamrich saw the importance of his inauguration in a "simplified and streamlined" ceremony. Invitations were limited to individuals and institutions connected with the state of Michigan. The televised event was held on the afternoon of October 14, 1969 in the Hedgcock Fieldhouse. At this inauguration, the medallion or chain of office and the mace were used for the first time. Two members of the Board of Trustees placed the medallion around the president's neck.

President Jamrich had the medallion or the chain of office, a silver-plated bronze circular disk, created by the Medallic Art Company of New York. It is worn at commencements and at other university functions on campus by the President. The first mace, a symbol of the authority of the university to grant degrees, was designed and created by Industrial Arts teacher Kauko A. Wahtera and his students in 1968-1969. It was first used at the 1969 inauguration. It is now carried by the senior faculty member at commencements. Both of these artifacts, created under the direction of Dr. Jamrich, enriched the traditions of the University.

Within a few years of his presidency, John Jamrich made it a point to celebrate Northern's 75th anniversary. He mandated that a celebration be held. Mariam Hilton was tapped as author for the first comprehensive history of the University entitled *Northern Michigan University, The First 75 Years*. There were a series of celebrations and a grand banquet to commemorate the event.

Less known is Jamrich's preservation of history in word and photograph. Down to the present time Jamrich maintains meticulous computer files from which he can retrieve an item within minutes. Today due to his foresight the NMU Archives contains hundreds of photographs showing every aspect of his years as president. No researcher is wanting for information on the Jamrich years.

Unfortunately during his years as president an official archives did not exist. He saw to it that monies were made available to microfilm Board minutes and related documents so that they would be preserved. They are now housed in the NMU Archives.

For the Northern centennial in 1999, he worked closely with the University Historian, Dr. Russell Magnaghi, and his expertise added to the event. It was John Jamrich who suggested the title for the encyclopedia, *A Sense of Time*. He also wrote a special musical composition and personally presented it to the university community. When Magnaghi's work as Upper Peninsula historian and retirement were celebrated in June 2014, Dr. Jamrich contributed an essay co-authored with President David Haynes for the festschrift. He also wrote an amusing composition, "Festschrift Ballad," to honor Magnaghi.

Over the decades since his retirement in 1983, Dr. Jamrich has maintained a strong connection with Northern Michigan University and the Upper Peninsula. On frequent summer visits, many made by rail and auto due to ear problems that prohibited air flight, he has visited with presidents, provided advice when asked, held special dinners for former administrators and faculty who worked with him, along with alumni, and friends.

President Jamrich developed a loyal staff. Some faculty from that time occasionally criticize this pattern. These individuals may not fully understand that a strong leader managing a large institution, dealing with thousands of people, programs, and problems, needs to know that he is backed by a loyal staff who will readily help him get all these tasks accomplished.

Back in the mid-1990s when Dr. Jamrich and June were invited to carry out an oral interview about their years at Northern, they provided many hours of reminiscences. These tapes and transcripts provide researchers with the story from his perspective, an important point of view. This provides an excellent working foundation for future biographical studies of the man and his times.

Jamrich has a subtle sense of humor and was a man of good humor as president. He tended to deal with tense situations in this fashion. He still does. Recently when he was 93 and asked if he planned to attend the dedication of the new Jamrich Hall he responded, "Yes. I will be there in person or looking across from Park Cemetery."

The Woman

June Jamrich supported her husband throughout his career, raising three daughters, Marna, June, and Barbara. On campus she was a gracious hostess. Their home was frequently open to staff, faculty and students, as well as the many guests who frequently arrived on campus.

June related in an interview, "at Northern I made every effort to relate to our students in a variety of ways. As can be expected, newly arrived students (freshmen or transfers) had to make the adjustment to the college setting and to Northern. Our home—Kaye House—was 'always open' to individual students or groups of students, for whatever reason they might want to come over." [53] She was also hostess for distinguished campus visitors, from congressmen, state legislators, governors, sports figures, and other national figures.

Mrs. Jamrich was the first wife of a president since Minnie Waldo in 1902 to hold a position at Northern. She was an ice skater who did recreational and competitive figure skating. When the regular instructor broke her leg, June took over the position with considerable enthusiasm.

Many Marquette and Upper Peninsula supporters came to Northern through the activities of the Presidents Club and the Development Fund, both organized for the purpose of raising funds for the University. Most of the fund-raising activities organized by June either took place at Kaye House or the University Center. June also was a member of several Marquette area organizations including the Fortnightly Club. She was also a member of the Faculty Wives and the U.S. Figure Skating Association.

"One of the supportive activities of our presidency was the area of music and the fine arts. We founded the Jamrich Piano/Music Scholarship, as well as establishing the Jamrich Art Endowment. The Art Endowment supports periodic art exhibits brought to campus."

June regularly accompanied the president to many of the other university functions such as athletic events. The most memorable series of trips was related to the football playoffs and the final game that brought the NCAA, Division II Football Championship to Northern Michigan University in 1975.

Among her Upper Peninsula recollections away from campus were their personal and family recreational activities, especially as they related to their cottage on Saux Head Lake and their 640 acres of forestland on County Road 510. With her memories of Northern Michigan University and the Upper Peninsula, Mrs. Jamrich thoroughly enjoys her return visits to the area. Usually she and John are gracious host and hostess to dinner parties for former staff and friends.

<u>Summary</u>

A number of major ingredients went into the Jamrich administration at Northern Michigan University.[54] There was his European heritage and growing up in Slovakia during the 1920s, which led him to stress culture and music, while at the same time showing him quite dramatically that progress in education was extremely important. Coupled with the cultural aspect was his academic career built on the sciences and mathematics and his view of the world and how Northern Michigan University would impact it. This concept is best summed up in the motto he developed for the University, "Putting tomorrow in good hands."

An extremely important component to the Jamrich story was his relationship with Michigan State University and with the previous president of Northern Michigan University Edgar Harden. President Harden had arrived in 1956 with the mandate from the state legislature to either close Northern or bring it into the mid-twentieth century by expanding its offerings and physical plant, and ultimately turning it into a university, all of which Harden did by 1963. When President Jamrich arrived in 1968 he used his strong abilities of organizing and forward-looking tied in with the Harden goals to turn Northern Michigan College into a university in fact as well as in name. President Jamrich used his skills and expertise to conduct this transformation. During the years of his administration President Jamrich used his scientific expertise to greatly expand the concept of the University on all levels. This was done in the turbulent 1960s and 1970s with the considerable distractions of the Civil Rights crisis and the Vietnam War. It was a new era when young just-minted faculty wanted shared governance and unionization, while administrators had developed around a different set of principles. Naturally there would be clashes between these two ideas. As a result the Jamrich years—1968-1983—were years of strained relations, development on all levels, physical plant construction, the development of new and exciting programs, and moving Northern Michigan University into the latter part of the twentieth century and beyond.

In typical Jamrich fashion he enlisted University personnel to devise the "Development Plan 1968-1980," within six months of his tenure on campus. This development plan was prepared in response to a request for such a document by the state legislature and other agencies interested in the rational development of higher education in Michigan. The plan, which was approved by the Board of Trustees, provided flexible guidelines for the orderly growth of the University's programs, staff, and facilities designed to meet its stated objectives.[55]

One of the goals accomplished by Jamrich most directly affecting students was a substantial lowering of the student-faculty ratio, while at the same time increasing the percentage of faculty with terminal degrees by more than 100 percent.

A number of student services and programs also were initiated for disadvantaged, handicapped, minorities, and those needing academic assistance. Program accessibility to the handicapped and barrier-free improvements were special goals of the president. For all of the students, financial aid was expanded to a point where Northern led all other state-assisted institutions in percentage of funds committed from the general fund.

Every aspect of Northern Michigan University today reflects the accomplishments of John X. Jamrich.

EPILOGUE

To conclude the biography Dr. Jamrich has agreed to provide an overview of his and June's retirement:

Retirement

John X. Jamrich

I want to underscore our personal, retrospective view of the years since retirement. If asked the usual question if we would do it over again, would it be different, we turn to the old cliché: "we would pursue the same activities and commitments" as our reply. And we add one other pertinent statement, namely, whatever the details might be, *the fact is that in retirement, the primary, significant attention revolves around providing the essentials of personal existence.*

June and I feel a sense of fervent satisfaction, joy, gratification, with a reverent feeling for the blessings that have been ours during those three decades: generally good health, genuine new friendships, retention of contact with our friends accumulated during our "professional years" in higher education, the formulation of new ventures, meeting new challenges, and the ultimate joy of a loving and caring family. We watch with gratification the career accomplishments of our three daughters and the interesting lives of our four grandchildren as they move into adulthood.

At the point of retirement, one makes decisions whether (1) to continue working; (2) quit completely the involvement in work related to the original career in pre-retirement years; (3) decide on a gradual withdrawal from the original career to a period of years that is a gradual withdrawal of a decade or so, turning in the meantime to identifying an entirely new configuration of activity, that however, contains a basic connection to many of the elements that were part of the years of the professional career. The latter might be referred to as the "decompression" phase of retirement.

After retirement, we opted to return to the Michigan State University area, specifically a home we purchased in Okemos, Michigan. That was not an easy decision to leave Marquette and Northern, but that is another "side-bar" story. The list begins here:

** Visiting lectures and informal consultation at Michigan State University

** Consultant to the State Department of Education in Lansing

** Board member of the Lansing Community Chest.

** Considerable golf with former MSU colleagues, two or three times per week; included luncheons; unable to shoot my age!

** Mrs. Jamrich became associated with the MSU Women's Golf Group, and served as an officer in that organization.

** Consultant to a law firm during our years in Okemos; the focus was on higher education and K-12 legal matters, especially Legislative activity related to the area of education; I still had friends among legislators and their staff members; also initiated a weekly bulletin for the attorneys.

** Informal "consultant" to legislators regarding higher education, with primary focus on Northern Michigan University at a time when legislative attitude indicated a need at that time. I joined with former President Harden in some of this informal activity.

** Mrs. Jamrich also had membership in the Okemos Women's Golf Association; she was a trophy winner several times.

** Served with Public Service Associates; that was a legislative lobby firm.

** As owners of a tract of forest land in the Marquette County area, we devoted considerable attention to timber growth and timber harvesting.

** During our years in the presidency, we purchased a Saux Head Lake frontage from Mrs. Kaufman at Loma Farms, and constructed a cottage that became a regular, summer place after retirement. The summers we spent at Saux Head after retirement are some of our fondest memories of the beauty of the U.P. Fishing, sailing, and swimming were part of the major activity during those years, plus entertaining our Marquette area friends and University colleagues.

** For quite a few years, Okemos continued to be our permanent residence. Living in the shadows of MSU, and in an excellent housing development was a joy.

** During the Okemos years, we revived our friendship with President and Mrs. Hannah; football games with them; picnics at their farm adjoining the MSU campus.

** During those years, with our three daughters residing in various parts of the country, we were active visitors to their places of residence, especially when there was a birth of a grandchild. Babysitting was a welcome activity.

** During the retirement years, we participated in ship cruises, especially when our daughter was teaching at the University in St. Thomas; and we celebrated a couple of our wedding anniversaries aboard cruise ships.

** Moved to Arizona from Okemos. Those turned out to be rather interesting years in the Scottsdale area. Of course, golf at one of the nation's premier courses had just opened; it was and is a difficult course; my neighbor and I were among the earliest players on the course; difficult? I would have to be Methuselah to "shoot my age." The most important factor actually related to Northern Michigan University and to the Upper Peninsula; a large number of the residents of Sun City were U.P. retirees, with quite a number of NMU graduates. Dr. Roy Heath, who served NMU as Vice President for Research during my tenure, resided in Sun City where he actually emerged as the leader and coordinator for many events related to the U.P. and Northern graduates, events that included outing, lectures, and alumni gatherings.

One of the important, NMU contacts was Bill and Gloria Jackson who had established a very substantial business in Arizona. Gloria (passed away recently) was an NMU graduate and a contributor to Northern; also, as one with a Finnish background, she provided considerable, financial and program support for

Suomi College. Her Northern contributions support a successful program for students to study overseas.

We also provided assistance to a graduate of Michigan State who was formulating plans to develop an extensive, retirement facility, especially for retired faculty and staff from colleges and universities.

As a resident of Fountain Hills, AZ, I became a member of the Fountain Hills Men's Club that provided very active times; my primary contribution was entertaining with piano music at the weekly dinners. Again, golf for me and Mrs. Jamrich continued to be an important part of our activity calendar.

Over time, since just after the War, fishing, for both my wife and for me had become one of our major activities; it all began with an early visit, after World War II to the U.P. at Lake Kawbawgam, and to a favorite fishing spot just across the border into Wisconsin. Canada was another fishing attraction for us.

Our years at Saux Head Lake and then the Dead River Basin (where our daughter and her husband built a Lodge) -- has served us as a summer time place to visit all these years. June and Dan are NMU alumni, successful authors of computer textbooks for many years.

In Arizona, we also were involved with the establishment of a new church. Additionally, we did occasional work at the Indian reservation nearby.

Also at this time, one of our daughters lived in El Paso. Our visits to their home included trips to the Mexican desert in search of arrow heads and pottery. And we took special time to be there at the birth of our grandchildren.

During our years in Fountain Hills, we continued as patients of Mayo Clinic; we were some of the early patients of the newly constructed, Mayo Clinic in Arizona. As of this year, we have been patients of Mayo clinic for over forty years. Some of the health care included several surgeries for both of us.

** While in Okemos, Mrs. Jamrich carried on research about Frederick Remington, the famous Western oil painter. She lectured frequently to various groups including schools.

** The move to Venice, Florida came next. There, including Sarasota, were quite a few NMU alumni as well as a visible number of U.P. retirees. Alumni gatherings were well attended; one of the leading organizers was Boots Kukuk, a native of the U.P.

** During our Venice residency of about 12 years, I spent considerable time as a volunteer at the Taylor elementary School, just across the street from the Plantation. They had an "in-school" TV station that broadcast news/sports and weather every day. As a professional meteorologist, my volunteer work was the instruction of the six or nine students who operated the TV station, and did the weather forecast. Over the years, students were rotated as TV operators and broadcasters.

** In Venice, Mrs. Jamrich served on the Board of Directors of the Plantation Community Foundation; this Foundation dispersed substantial dollars each year to the Women's Center, Teen-age Court, the Wild-life Center, and Taylor Elementary School, to list a few of the recipients.

** Also, during those Venice years, I was commissioned to write the history of the Plantation in Venice; this was a two-golf course, extensive housing development. I also wrote the history of the Foundation.

** We enjoyed the time we spent in Venice and Sarasota with their excellent programs in the Arts and music. The Venice Senior Social Center was quite a fantastic service for senior citizens of the area. Dinner was served every evening; twice per week I would entertain with piano music.

** Of course, as we aged, attention continued to our health and general welfare.

** And, I continued to compose music: several piano works, solo voice and choir music for churches, as well as performing in some of the local churches. The Northern Michigan University Board of Trustees commissioned me to compose the NMU Centennial Suite that was performed during the Centennial Program at the University. In addition, I did numerous compositions for birthdays and anniversaries of friends.

** Then, giving consideration to the proximity of the Mayo Clinic now with a clinic and hospital in Jacksonville, Florida, we decided to move to Jacksonville. The Retirement facility – Cypress village – that we selected is within walking distance of the Clinic and Hospital.

** Golf was a major activity until just a few years ago. I was designated as Pianist in Residence at the Mayo Clinic, now having performed there several times each week for more than eleven years; that amounts to a total of 1,360 one-hour recitals in the Mayo Patient Lounge. Add to that the time we devoted to writing the family history – prose and photos – and including a complete family genealogy. And, we continue our contacts with Northern, Northwestern University, Ripon College, Coe College, Marquette University; I received an Honorary Degree from Grand Valley State University acknowledging the significant role my Legislative Survey of the Grand Rapids area resulted in the establishment of Grand Valley State University.

** Other activities in Venice: Board member of the Board of Governors of the Plantation; on the Governing Boards of Harrington Lake Association; for the latter, I provided piano/organ music at the regular, Tuesday evening Association dinners. Mrs. Jamrich was an active member of the Plantation Women's Golf Association, and winner of several trophies.

** Mrs. Jamrich and I traveled not just in the U.S. to visit our family and friends, but also to Israel, Mexico, Canada, and Slovakia.

**Here at Cypress Village, Mrs. Jamrich has served as Unit Leader in the general organization; she has been active in organizing many social events such as Christmas parties, spring picnics, etc. and now organized a Canasta Club.

** Fishing is still a favorite activity. Cypress village has several lakes that are excellent sources of fishing activity.

** In Venice: Mrs. Jamrich organized and choreographed an excellent and extensive dance program involving about two dozen dancers. She also became an ardent fan of orchid plants.

** Mrs. Jamrich has devoted considerable time to the preparation of about 35 photo albums that preserve visual evidence of our lifetime.

** My compilation of the special composition, "Festschrift Ballad" for Russ Magnaghi's Festschrift Event, June 4, 2014.

APPENDIX I: REPORTS AND PUBLICATIONS

1. "Teaching Materials," *Review of Educational Research*, (1951).

2. "Evaluation in College Teaching and Administration," *North Central Association Quarterly* (1955).

3. "Organizational Practices in Student Faculty Counseling Programs," *North Central Association Quarterly* (1955).

4. Report of the Michigan Survey of Higher Education:

   Staff Study No. 6, *Instructional Programs in Michigan Institutions of Higher Education,* by John Dale Russell, John X. Jamrich, and Orvin T. Richardson. March 1958.

   Staff Study No. 8, *Financial Assistance to Students in Michigan Institutions of Higher Education,* by John X. Jamrich. May 1958.

   Staff Study No. 9, *Space Utilization and Value of Physical Plants in Michigan Institutions of Higher Education*, by John Dale Russell and John X. Jamrich. June 1958.

   Staff Study No. 10, *Faculties of the Michigan Institutions of Higher Education*, by John X. Jamrich. June 1958.
   (also coordinated the other 13 reports of the Survey.)

5. *New College*, 1958. (Report on Survey of educational needs in the Grand Rapids area.)

   a. *Latin American Higher Education and Inter-American Cooperation.* (OAS document)
   b. "Research Techniques in State Surveys of Higher Education," *College and University*, Sept. 1960.
   c. *Survey of Physical Facilities in Colleges and Universities of New York State*, 1960.

    d. *Analysis of Income and Expenditure in New York Institutions of Higher Education*, 1960.

    e. *Graduate Programs in New York Institutions of Higher Education*, 1960.

    f. *Evaluation in Higher Education*, (one chapter), ed. Paul Dressel (1960).

6. "Application of Matrices in the Analysis of Sociometric Data," in *Journal of Experimental Education* (1960).

7. Contributor, *Issues in Higher Education*, 1959, 1960, 1961.

8. "Research Techniques in State Surveys," *College and University Business*, Sept. 1960.

9. "The Use and Planning of Instructional Facilities in Small Colleges," *North Central Association Quarterly* (Jan. 1961).

10. *Problems of New Faculty Members in Colleges and Universities*. Michigan State University, 1961.

11. *Utilization of Instructional Facilities at the University of Chicago*, 1961.

12. *Utilization of Instructional Facilities and an Inventory of Physical Plants in the State Controlled Institutions of Higher Education in Michigan*. 1961.

13. "Soviet and U. S. Images of Teachers," *School and Society*, Sept. 1961.

14. "Investing in Higher Education," The Michigan Economic

Record, Nov. 1961.

15. "Higher Education," *The Michigan State University Magazine*, Jan. 1961.

16. *Educational Needs in Latin American*, HE: CHEAR, Dec. 1961.

17. Position Paper on Education for Michigan Gov. George Romney.

18. "Higher Education in Michigan: Critical Decade Ahead," *Challenge*. Michigan State Chamber of Commerce, Jan. 1963.

19. *To Build or Not To Build: The Use and Planning of Instructional Facilities in Higher Education*. Educational Facilities Laboratory, 1962.

20. "Improvement of Instruction in Higher Education," AACTE Study Series No. 6, 1962.

21. *Higher Education Needs in the Saginaw Valley*, Survey conducted for the Michigan Legislature, Nov. 1962.

22. *Capital Outlay Needs for the State Controlled Institutions in Ohio: 1962-72*. Study prepared for the Ohio Legislature, 1963.

23. *Problems of New Faculty in Community Colleges* (co-author), 1963.

24. *The University of Nigeria: A Development Program*, Report to the Ford Foundation. "Inter-Institutional Cooperation in Research and Instruction," *College and University*, Fall 1964.

25. "A Basic Plan Needed for Higher Education," *Michigan Education Journal*, January 1965.

26. *Physical Facilities in Virginia's Higher Education*, 1965.

27. *Doctorates in Education*, Report to the Ohio Board of Regents, 1965.

28. *Physical Facilities in Michigan Higher Education*, 1966.

29. "Control of Higher Education," *Encyclopedia of Educational Research*, 1968.

30. *Development Plan 1968-1980*, Northern Michigan University, 1968.

31. *President's Report of Progress*, NMU 1970, 1973.

32. with David Haynes. "Northern Michigan University and the Upper Peninsula," in Robert Archibald, editor. *Northern Border: History and Lore of Michigan's Upper Peninsula and Beyond.* Marquette: Northern Michigan University Press, 2014.

APPENDIX II: MEMBERSHIPS

Listed in: Who's Who in America

    Who's Who in Education

    American Men of Science

    Who's Who in the Midwest

American Association for the Advancement of Science (Fellow)

American Personnel and Guidance Association

American Mathematics Society

Phi Delta Kappa

American Educational Research Association

Association for Higher Education

Michigan Association of the Professions

American Association of State Colleges and Universities (Committee on Research)

Michigan Council for the Arts (Appointed by Gov. Milliken 1969)

Operation Action U. P.

Upper Peninsula Committee for Area Progress (UPCAP)

APPENDIX III: OTHER ACTIVITIES

1. Consultant to colleges on administration, program and finance.

2. Accreditation visitor—North Central Association of Colleges and Secondary Schools.

3. Speaker, National Institutional Research Forum (1963), Northern Illinois University Institutional Research Conference (1963), and similar conferences.

4. AERA Program, 1961, 1962.

5. Consultant and Speaker, Conference of Higher Education of the National Committee of the Churches of Christ, 1962.

6. Main Speaker at New England Board of Higher Education Workshop on Institutional Research, 1962.

7. Main Speaker at Annual Session of Council for the Advancement of Small Colleges, 1962.

8. Consultant, Michigan Constitutional Convention Education Committee.

9. Member, Michigan Education Association Constitutional Seminar, 1962.

10. Consultant, Michigan Council of State College Presidents.

11. Speaker, Rotary Clubs: Lansing, Grand Rapids, East Lansing, Iron Mountain, Marquette.

12. Speaker, annual PTA clinics.

13. Commencement Speaker: Grand Rapids Junior College, Lansing Community College, Alpena Community College.

14. Accreditation visits for Michigan Department of Public Instruction.

15. Secretary-Treasurer, Nebraska Association of College and Universities, 1955-57.

16. Director of Church Choirs and Conductor of Cudahy Municipal Band.

17. Service Club Memberships: Lions, Cedar Rapids, Iowa; Rotary, Crete, Nebraska; Cedar Rapids Junior Chamber of Commerce; Crete Chamber of Commerce; Marquette Chamber of Commerce.

18. Chairman, Conference on Nuclear Power, 1955-56.

19. Organizer of Association of Midwest Conference of Personnel Deans, 1953.

20. Member, Board of Trustees, St. Luke's Hospital, Marquette.

21. Member, Board of Directors, Bay Cliff Health Camp, Marquette.

22. Member, Board of Directors, Lake Superior and Ishpeming Railroad Company.

23. Travel: Africa, Thailand, Czechoslovakia, Russia, Mexico, Finland, Italy, Israel.

24. HEGIS Conference, 1971.

25. AASCU Summer Program, 1971.

26. Director, private college finance study, Virginia Commission on Higher Education.

27. Carthage College Board of Trustees, 1972.

28. Education Advisory Committee, U. S. Army Command and General Staff College, 1972-75.

29. Chairman, Committee on Studies, AASCU, 1972-74.

30. Speaker, National Conference on Rural Development, 1973.

31. Member, Michigan Bicentennial Commission (1972-75).

32. Member, Federal Advisory Council on Financial Aid to Students, 1974; Chairman, 1975-1976.

33. Member, American Council on Education, Commission on Administrative Affairs, 1974-83.

34. Member, Executive Committee, Operation Action U.P., 1968-73.

35. Member Newcomen Society of North America, 1974-83.

36. AASCU Program, 1974.

37. Member, National Advisory Council, National Center for Higher Education Management Systems, 1975.

38. Board of Directors, Harrington Lake Association and Governor's Green Association of Plantation Golf & Country Club, Venice, FL.

39. Author, *History of the Plantation Golf & Country Club*.

40. Volunteer pianist, retirement communities, Venice and Sarasota, FL.

41. Volunteer pianist and Pianist in Residence, Mayo Clinic, Jacksonville, FL.

APPENDIX IV: AWARDS

Russian military citation for service to USSR Air Force, 1945

Honorary degree (Humane Letters), Northern Michigan University, 1968

Israel City of Peace Award, 1974

Order of the Lion, Finland, 1975

Distinguished Alumni Award, Ripon College, 1983

Honorary degree from Grand Valley State University, 1985

APPENDIX V: REMEMBERING THE MAN

Although this work has relied on the memories of numerous people through oral interviews, what follows are a number of lengthier reminiscences of John X. Jamrich by a variety of people who worked with him and directly felt the effects of his personality.

Dr. Clifford Maier was Professor of History and NMU's first archivist (1983-1992) and well remembers Dr. Jamrich's assistance in starting a very embryonic archival program which led to the present archive: It was around 1976 when Russ Magnaghi wrote a letter directly to Dr. Jamrich promoting the idea of a resource room or small archive to house materials he had gathered relating to Northern and the Upper Peninsula. Dr. Jamrich forwarded the letter to Provost Robert Glenn and as a result a small space was awarded with some basic archival equipment. This started the process. Dr. Ruth Roebke-Berens, chair of the History Department followed by opening talks with Martha Bigelow, director the State History Division concerning the development of a state archive branch on the NMU campus. She in turn was supported by the department and by the time Dr. Jamrich retired in 1983, the NMU Archive was in place and its growth was underway.

R. Tom Peters was an alum of Northern was the assistant to President Jamrich and remembers: President Jamrich was an excellent leader and administrator. He surrounded himself with loyal and competent people and let them do their jobs without interference, but with a great deal of support when needed.

He was very active in his support of the total Athletic program at Northern while working through Title IX, Conference affiliations, a National Championship in Football, and the start of the Ice Hockey program. As a former weatherman in the Army Air Force, he constantly observed the weather forecast prior to home football games, years before we had the Superior Dome, and made sure that the field was covered if the weather looked bad. It was not uncommon to get a call at 4:00 p.m. on a Friday from the President suggesting we put the tarp down on the field as bad weather was coming. In addition, he was most supportive of the Golden Wildcat Club and its support of athletics and the formation of the Blue Line Club to support the new Ice Hockey program. He and Mrs. Jamrich were frequently in attendance at the Club functions as well in attendance at all of the various athletic contests.

President Jamrich was effective in his dealings with the State Legislature making sure that Northern got its fair share of appropriations and Capital Outlay projects. His strong relationship with State Representative Dominic Jacobetti and State Senator Joe Mack went a long way to making sure that Northern was well cared for in the budget process.

President Jamrich was also very prominent in the Alumni and Development activities of the University. He was very effective in his role with donors and was in attendance at most Alumni meetings and activities throughout the country. He was a big supporter of the NMU Fantastics and the Arts Chorale as they traveled around the State and country promoting Northern in a most positive manner. John X. Jamrich – a President for all seasons!

Eric Smith, long –time director of Broadcasting and Audio Visual Services in the Learning Resources Center brought to light an interesting and relatively little known aspect of the Jamrich story: In the 1970s George Lott in charge of television programing was called to President Jamrich's office one day. Jamrich was familiar with national television's College Bowl and wanted George to develop a similar experience on campus. At the president's urging and promoting, Lott got to work and created NMU's High School Bowl. This program continues to the present day and is WNMU-TV's longest running program and one of the most popular. It has provided scholarships for many students and has attracted thousands of students to Northern who first arrived on buses as contestants or the audience. It is another example of Dr. Jamrich's direct involvement with the operation of the University.

Karen and Jack Kunkel first came to campus just prior to President Jamrich's arrival and remained during his administration. Jack served in the Housing office and Karen was a ski instructor and then director of the Olympic Training Center. As Karen remembers: I have a book of wonderful memories of the man. When Title IX was being implemented Dr. Jamrich gave Barb Patrick total support, unfortunately she is presently too ill to give an interview. I was put in charge of the development of the Olympic Training Center. There were many naysayers who thought the Center was a waste of time and money, so besides working to develop the Center which was a challenge, I had to deal with this faction. Always there to support me was Dr. Jamrich and the result was the successfully development of the Center. At an earlier juncture the University was being sued because a student I was teaching on the ski slopes had broken both legs. From start to finish I had the complete support of the President Jamrich and Northern won the case. This support was important because at the time I was relatively new on the faculty, we had a growing family, and this was a terrible event to have to face with serious financial implications.

Jack also has fond memories of working with President Jamrich: Soon after I arrived I was put in charge of the Housing office. At the time campuses were alive with student and faculty unrest and protests. President Jamrich was on top of most everything that went unfolded on campus. He told me I had his support in Housing, get the job done, but I was accountable to him in the end. As a result I must say he was the best boss I ever worked for and I was able to get the job done. This is an interesting story connected with Dr. Jamrich's concern for student affairs. One night a group of male students went on a panty raid on Carey Hall. When I arrived I saw Dr. Jamrich on the margins of the crowd and joined him and some other administrators. All of a sudden I looked over toward Jamrich and saw that he had a panty draped on his shoulder. What do I do? I colleague who also saw what happened told me to quickly grab the panty before he saw it and put it into my pocket, which I did. I could recount many other similar incidents. Despite such situations, Dr. Jamrich never shied away from trouble on campus, making sure that he was directly aware of what was happening and could take immediate action to diffuse the trouble.

As we have seen time and time again, Dr. Jamrich remained aware of most of the important happenings on campus. Russ Magnaghi, professor of History remembers an interesting and unexpected incident: I was invited to a breakfast for President Gerald Ford when he visited campus in November 1978 attended by a dozen or more people. I had just begun to develop my interest and work on the Upper Peninsula and had no idea that Dr. Jamrich was aware of this. I wondered why I was invited to this breakfast. Well I soon got the answer. We were all sitting down prior to the food being served when President Jamrich turned to me and asked me to fill-in the former president on the history of the Upper Peninsula. Then in about five minutes I gave my survey history to the 38th president of the United States.

Finally there is the observation make by Gene Whitehouse, the associate dean of Arts and Sciences during the Jamrich years: One day a group of faculty members was talking about President Jamrich's impending retirement in 1983. They were in agreement that he had stayed too long, it was time that he go, and his replacement would be new and better. Hearing this I pointed out to them that they knew the president they had, but they should not be so sure that the future president would be as good as Dr. Jamrich had been.

From what has been presented here by Dr. Whitehouse his observation has been proven correct.

Notes:

[1] John X. Jamrich. "Our Family Circle: Biographical/Historical Monograph," (2008), p. 38. This 251-page unpublished compilation provides remarkable details into the early life of the Jamrich family. It can be found in the "Jamrich Papers" in the NMU Archives.

[2] Jamrich. "Our Family Circle," p. 79.

[3] Jamrich. "Our Family Circle," p. 78.

[4] John X. Jamrich to Russell M. Magnaghi, October 21, 2013, "Jamrich Papers," NMU Archives.

[5] Jamrich. "Our Family Circle," p. 85.

[6] Jamrich. "Our Family Circle," pp 26-27.

[7] Jamrich. "Our Family Circle," p; 28.

[8] Jamrich. "Our Family Circle," p. 85.

[9] Jamrich. "Our Family Circle," p. 67-68.

[10] Jamrich described this experience in a typescript titled "I Was Part of a U. S. – Soviet Honeymoon; undated, 7 pages, pp. 3-5. Deposited in the "Jamrich Papers, NMU Archives.

[11] Jamrich provided more details about this tricky situation in a lengthy letter to an information specialist at Fort Wainwright, Alaska, in October of 2005 see: Jamrich. "Our Family Circle," pp. 49-56.

[12] Jamrich. "Our Family Circle," pp. 51-52.

[13] Jamrich. "Our Family Circle," p. 105.

[14] Jamrich. "Our Family Circle," p. 140.

[15] Jamrich. "Our Family Circle," p. 142

[16] Jamrich. "Our Family Circle," p. 145.

[17] Jamrich. "Our Family Circle," p. 145.

[18] Seidman, educated at Dartmouth, Harvard, and the University of Michigan, moved from his family's accounting business into government service, eventually as Director of the Federal Deposit Insurance Corporation, where he most notably helped stabilize the Savings & Loan Crisis, an accomplishment for which he was cashiered by the administration of fellow Republican, President George H. W. Bush.

[19] Jamrich. "Our Family Circle," p. 153.

[20] Jamrich. "Our Family Circle," p. 157.

[21] Jamrich. "Our Family Circle," p. 228.

²² Jamrich. "Our Family Circle," p. 44.

²³ Jamrich. "Our Family Circle," p. 71.

²⁴ Jamrich. "Our Family Circle," p. 237.

²⁵ Jamrich. "Our Family Circle," pp. 176-177 and Jamrich. "McClellan Had It In for Me" [2013], Magnaghi Papers, NMU Archives.

²⁶ See: Academic *Negotiations: Alternatives to Collective Bargaining*. Chicago, March 1967, p. 2 and Mariam Hilton. *Northern Michigan University, The First 75 Years.* Marquette: Northern Michigan University Press, 1975, p 199.

²⁷ Hilton. *75 Years*, pp. 209-210.

²⁸ *Development Plan, 1968-80*. Marquette: Northern Michigan University, 1969.

²⁹ Northern was accredited by the following: The National Council for the Accreditation of Teacher Education, The American Chemical Society, The American Medical Association Council on Medical Education and Hospitals, the American Speech and Hearing Association, The Certified Laboratory Assistant Association, The National Association of Schools of Music, the Council on Social Work Education, and the Board of Nursing of the State of Michigan.

³⁰ *Northern Michigan University Bulletin, 1969-1970*, pp. 282-299; these figures are a bit unreliable because there are degrees which may or may not been terminal in a field.

³¹ *Northern Michigan University Undergraduate Bulletin, 1982-1984*, pp. 217-227.

³² The University Archives has extensive files dealing with faculty research that can be consulted under "Faculty Research Grants, University Series 8, 11, 72."

³³ Marcus Robyns and Carrie Fries. "The Battle for Shared Governance: The Northern Michigan University Chapter of the American Association of University Professors, 1967 to 1976." *Michigan Historical Review* 28:2 (Fall 2002), 1-41; see also *Blood on the Table: The Birth of the Northern Michigan University Chapter of the American Association of University Professors, 1967-1976.* Marquette: AAUP, {no date], p. 1.

³⁴ Oral history with Donald Heikkinen, July 29, 1994, NMU Archives.

³⁵ Robyns and Fries. *Michigan Historical Review*..

[36] Jamrich to Magnaghi, August 6, 2014, Magnaghi Papers, NMU Archives.

[37] Magnaghi. *A Sense of Time,* p. 62.

[38] Much of the detail here comes from oral interview with David McClintock, 1995 deposited in NMU Archives.

[39] Oral interview with R. Thomas Peters, Assistant to the President, July 18, 1994, NMU Archives.

[40] For specific information on the buildings see, Russell M. Magnaghi. *A Sense of Place: The Encyclopedia of Northern Michigan University*. Marquette: NMU Press in conjunction with the Center for UP Studies, 1999, pp. 245-246; 125-126; 234-235; 74; 312-313; 230-; 323-324.

[41] For an excellent review of the Admissions Office during the Jamrich years see: interviews with Jack Kunkel, July 29, 2014 and Martin Dolan, December 13, 2013, NMU Archives.

[42] *Northern Campus Review,* Summer 1973.

[43] *Northern News Review,* October-November 1973.

[44] See interview with Norman Hefke, April 7, 1995, NMU Archives.

[45] Interview with Norman Hefke, August 7, 2014, Magnaghi Papers, NMU Archives.

[46] Interview with Robert Archibald, August 8, 2014, Magnaghi Papers, NMU Archives.

[47] *Northern News-Review,* February 1982.

[48] Interview with Ken Chant, April 6, 1995 in the NMU Archives.

[49] The issues of *Northern News-Review,* for February – December 1982 provide the administration's view of the financial crisis. Stories also appear in *The North Wind* March 4, 1982 and in following issues through 1983.

[50] Jamrich to Magnaghi, August 6, 2014, Magnaghi Papers, NMU Archives.

[51] *The North Wind,* April 21, 1983.

[52] Robert F. McClellan to John X. Jamrich, April 17, 1981, "Jamrich Papers," NMU Archives.

[53] See "Our Family Circle," pp. 164-175 for an autobiographical interview.

[54] This study is based on: Interviews with John X. Jamrich,

deposited in the NMU Archives conducted in 1994, 2011; Miriam Hilton. *Northern Michigan University: The First 75 Years.* Marquette: Northern Michigan University Press, 1975; Russell M. Magnaghi. *A Sense of Time: The Encyclopedia of Northern Michigan University.* Marquette: Northern Michigan University Press and the Center for Upper Peninsula Studies, 1999.

[55] *Development Plan 1968/1980.*

BIBLIOGRAPHY

Development Plan, 1968-80. Marquette: Northern Michigan University, 1969.

Hilton, Mariam. *Northern Michigan University, The First 75 Years.* Marquette: Northern Michigan University Press, 1975.

Jamrich, John X. "Our Family Circle: Biographical/Historical Monograph," (2008). NMU Archives.

Magnaghi, Russell M. *A Sense of Place: The Encyclopedia of Northern Michigan University*. Marquette: Northern Michigan University Press in conjunction with the Center for UP Studies, 1999.

Northern Michigan University Undergraduate Bulletins, (1969 to 1983), NMU Archives.

Robyns, Marcus and Carrie Fries. "The Battle for Shared Governance: The Northern Michigan University Chapter of the American Association of University Professors, 1967 to 1976." *Michigan Historical Review* 28:2 (Fall 2002), 1-41.